SAIL the SPIRIT

SAIL
the
SPIRIT

Iain Sharp

REED

Sail the Spirit has been published with the assistance of The Spirit of Adventure Trust and Sanford Ltd. Sanford Ltd's wholly-owned subsidiary, Vos & Brijs shipyards, built *Spirit of Adventure* and subsequently has contributed significantly to the ongoing maintenance of both *Spirit of Adventure* and *Spirit of New Zealand*.

Published by Reed Books, a division of Reed Publishing (NZ) Ltd,
39 Rawene Road, Birkenhead, Auckland 10, New Zealand.
Associated companies, branches and representatives throughout the world.

ISBN 0 7900 0361 9

Text © Iain Sharp 1994
Interviews with Graham Weakley and Rosemary Parkin
© Tessa Duder 1994
Photographs © The Spirit of Adventure Trust,
except where credited otherwise
Line drawings © Steve Lampard and Gavin McLean

First published 1994

Designed by Susan Johnson
Typesetting and layout by Pressgang
Printed in Australia by Griffin Press

Contents

Acknowledgements

Everyone I met connected with The Spirit of Adventure Trust, from the chairman, Stephen Fisher, through to the youngest trainees, went out of their way to help me and I am deeply indebted to them all. It's fair to say, though, that without the assistance of certain people this book would not exist at all. In particular, I must thank Stephen Fisher for so generously making time available for me in his busy schedule; trustees Tessa and John Duder for interesting me in the project in the first place and supplying much of my basic information; the trust's chief executive, Bill McCook, for his unflagging good humour and encouragement, and for letting me cart off his files for long periods of time; the national fundraiser, Vaughan Robertson, for coming to my aid on dozens of occasions, including a couple of major computer breakdowns; the senior master, Paul Leppington, and the permanent master, Steve Gamble, for putting up so cheerfully with my landlubberly questions; Captain Barry Thompson, for reading my manuscript with such care (any remaining errors, I hasten to add, are my own); and all of the staff at the Marsden Wharf office for their patience and goodwill. On the subject of patience, I must also express my gratitude to my family, who had to endure my authorial grumpiness; and to Deirdre Parr, my long-suffering editor at Reed. I'm obliged, too, to my friend Joy MacKenzie for the loan of a typewriter at a crucial point and for her support throughout.

In the March issue of the trust's quarterly magazine, *The Spirit*, I advertised for help with photographic material. The response was overwhelming, and I thank everyone who took the trouble to send me photographs, many of which have been used to illustrate the text. Hanimex NZ Ltd kindly assisted by contributing film towards additional photographs commissioned from photographer Roy Emerson by The Spirit of Adventure Trust.

IAIN SHARP
JULY 1994

Editorial Note

The abbreviations SOA (*Spirit of Adventure*) and SONZ (*Spirit of New Zealand*) are used in the captions to indicate the ship that each voyage number relates to.

Foreword by
H.R.H. The Prince Edward, C.V.O.

BUCKINGHAM PALACE

There are few better experiences for anybody, especially young people, to learn more about themselves, others and nature than at sea. Cooped up in a small, confined space and at the mercy of whatever the elements may throw at you, suddenly you are faced with a matter of survival. More importantly, that survival depends upon knowing yourself, knowing your shipmates and knowing what to do when the weather changes.

For 21 years the STS *Spirit of Adventure* and STS *Spirit of New Zealand* between them have been consistently providing those sorts of experiences to young and old, able and not so able-bodied alike. This book provides a wonderful opportunity to share the experiences of a few of literally hundreds who have taken sail training on board one or other of these vessels. I can still vividly remember the few days I spent on board the *Spirit of Adventure* back in 1982, as too will my shipmates, though probably for different reasons!

Inevitably, like any trust or charitable body, it tends to be the worthier elements which are always expounded. We tend to forget to mention all the other vital seamanship skills that need to be taught or, for that matter, that sailing is fun, exhilarating, adventurous and sometimes scary. But then again, that is exactly what attracts people to the sport and it is much easier to learn when you are having fun.

I would like to congratulate and thank all those involved with The Spirit of Adventure Trust and wish them and all who sail with them in the future a fair wind and a kind sea.

Edward

1994

7

The Spirit of Adventure

The culture that has become The Spirit of Adventure Trust is well stated in Priest's *Adventure Experience Model* (1985):

> *A high skill level with low risk spells boredom. Nothing is gained, little is learnt and repeats are few.*
>
> *Alternatively, a low skill level with high risks spells misadventure or worse. Fear dominates and swamps any value in the activity.*
>
> *Match the two and we have adventure.*

Add our own special third ingredient, the *Spirits*, and you have our formula: the Spirit of Adventure. This, then, becomes the means to an end that we strive to accomplish, best described by Marcel Proust:

> *The real voyage of discovery consists not in seeking new lands, but in seeing them with new eyes.*

Stephen B. Fisher

Stephen B. Fisher QSO
Chairman, The Spirit of Adventure Trust

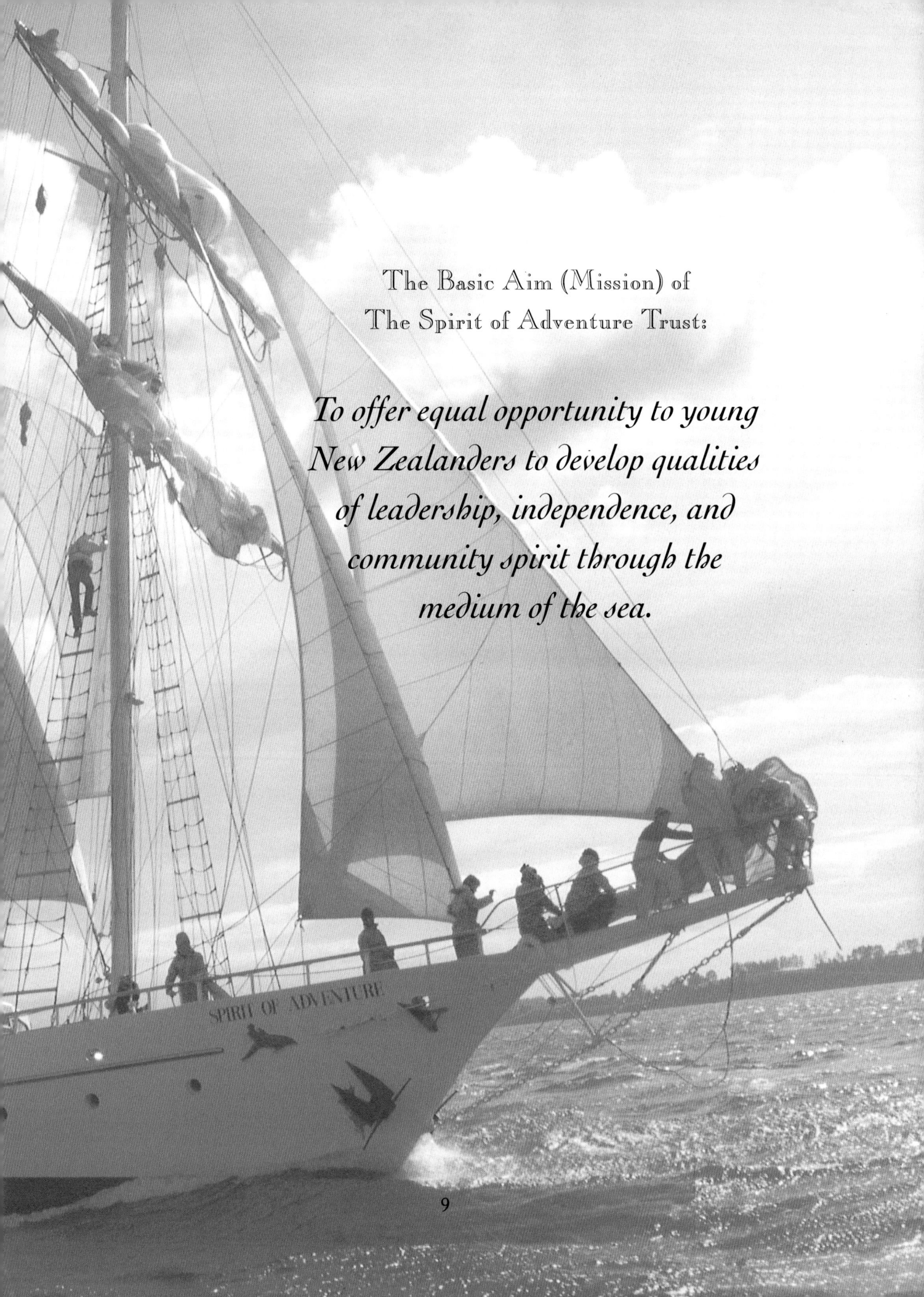

The Basic Aim (Mission) of
The Spirit of Adventure Trust:

*To offer equal opportunity to young
New Zealanders to develop qualities
of leadership, independence, and
community spirit through the
medium of the sea.*

9

Preface:
A Generosity of Spirit

B ut I don't know the first thing about sailing!' I blurted when Tessa Duder first suggested to me, in October 1992, that I might like to write a book about the *Spirit of Adventure* and *Spirit of New Zealand*. I was not exaggerating my ignorance. On either side of my family tree, I come from a long line of landlubbers. By October 1992 I had found out that boats have a sharp end, called the prow or bow or something like that, and a blunt end, called the stern. I was also aware that sailors referred to one side of their vessels as starboard and the other as port, but I could not remember which was which. My nautical acumen extended no further.

I had heard of the two *Spirit* ships, like almost everyone else in New Zealand, and I knew some people whose teenage children had sailed on them. I was hazy about the ships' purpose, however, except that it was somehow educational. I had no idea how the ships were administered, where they sailed, how long the voyages usually lasted, how many young people were likely to be aboard at any given time, or how many officers were required to supervise them. I had never seen either vessel up close.

My ignorance, Tessa assured me, would actually be an advantage. 'You'll be on exactly the same footing as 90 per cent of the trainees, who are as new to sailing as you are,' she said. 'So you'll be able to see things from their perspective. It's not the primary intention of The Spirit of Adventure Trust to produce crackerjack sailors anyway. What we're really interested in is the psychological development of young people. Sailing is the means rather than the end.'

The *Spirit of Adventure* and *Spirit of New Zealand* take high school pupils from the fifth, sixth and seventh forms on ten-day voyages and teach them the rudiments of good seamanship. They learn how to identify the different parts of the rigging, how to hoist and handle sails, how to weigh anchor, how to steer and how to read charts and compasses. Shorter voyages, including weekend excursions, help adult groups acquire or renew the same range of skills. But the main objectives of The Spirit of Adventure Trust have always been social rather than professional. The general idea is that, provided there is a basic willingness to participate and learn, even a short time aboard a sailing ship can help build up people's self-confidence and contribute significantly to their self-knowledge.

Tessa and her husband, John, have been closely associated with the Trust for many years. They were present when the *Spirit of Adventure* was launched in December 1973. They have sailed on both ships many times as volunteer officers (although rarely on the same voyages). A fine seaman, like many of his forebears in the seafaring Duder family, John was appointed to the trust board in October 1975. He was the principal author of the

Opposite: *The* Spirit of New Zealand *in Army Bay, Whangaparaoa Peninsula.*

11

Instructor's Handbook which was published by the trust in October 1977. Tessa became a trustee in September 1992, after more than a decade's service as a seemingly indefatigable committee member of the Volunteer Crew Association. She edited the trust's quarterly magazine, *The Spirit*, from its first issue in September 1986 until August 1990.

Tessa is also a prize-winning author of novels for older children; by the end of 1992, she was having trouble finding time for all the claims on her attention. In 1985, she compiled a meticulous history of the trust, with the assistance of maritime historian Clifford Hawkins and Captain Barry Thompson (one of the trust's founding members). There had been some major developments since then, including the launching of the *Spirit of New Zealand* in February 1986, but Tessa was too busy with other writing projects to undertake an update. That's why, with the trust's twenty-first anniversary approaching, she wanted to know if I would be interested in the task.

I agreed, mainly because I was curious to find out more about the process of psychological development Tessa had outlined. In the 1990s, body building is a more fashionable topic for discussion than character building. Afraid of seeming prim, cobwebbed and hopelessly uncool in the age of grunge, rap and heavy metal, most people tend to avoid such terms as 'character building' and 'moral education' nowadays, unless these have been coated first with a heavy layer of irony. Yet it's surely not a frivolous matter to inquire what kind of values we ought to pass on to the generations who come after us.

Over the last 18 months, I have met a large number of people connected, in one way or another, with The Spirit of Adventure Trust. These folk come in all shapes, sizes, ages and temperaments, but they share two qualities which I respect.

The first is generosity. Stephen Fisher, the trust's chairman since 1977, is a busy man with a large company to run. Yet, for many years, at the expense of his own leisure time, he has devoted the equivalent of two full working days per week to raising enough funds to ensure that young people throughout New Zealand (most of whom he will never meet) have the opportunity to go on sailing expeditions without paying prohibitive fees. His commitment sets the standard for the rest of the organisation. While it's true that the ships' permanent crew and the staff at the Operations Office are salaried positions, it's also fair to say that the officers put in many unpaid hours beyond the call of duty and they could make more money for less labour elsewhere. Nobody works for the trust just for financial gain; they have to believe in the overall philosophy of the youth development programme, because the rewards, if I may be allowed a bad pun, are chiefly spiritual. The 400 or so members of the Volunteer Crew Association receive no monetary remuneration for their services on voyages. Then there are all the fund-raisers, well-wishers and benefactors. Over the years, thousands of New Zealanders have donated money, time and goods to keep the trust's training programmes going.

There was a dark period in the middle of the 1980s, before the 1987 stock market crash brought an end to many rapacious dreams, when all-out greed threatened to become the predominant business ethic. Corporate raiders and asset strippers were suddenly folk heroes, with their wily features gracing (or disgracing) the covers of glossy magazines. To dollar-crazed eyes, it no longer mattered how diseased the methods were, as long as the bank balance looked healthy enough at the end of the day. With the accent on giving rather than taking, The Spirit of Adventure Trust is the antithesis, I believe, of the asset-stripping approach to life.

The other shared quality I admire in the trust's personnel and supporters is their conviction that personal integrity still counts for something in this world and that it always will.

Without needing to spell anything out in bold letters, they usually succeed in passing this conviction on to the young trainees.

According to the *Instructor's Handbook*, the principal aims of the trust's training programmes are 'the realisation of an individual's potential by physical and mental extension, the development of self-discipline and initiative, the development of proper qualities of leadership, tolerance and independence by living and working in a community'; in other words, to help young people get more out of themselves so that they can put more into life and society. To some ears, words like 'discipline', 'initiative', 'proper', 'leadership' and even 'development' might have a disagreeably puritanical ring. As I've already noted, it's not easy to talk about character building nowadays without sounding rather stern and dated. But the kind of character the trust is trying to build is not that of a puritan. Quite the reverse. Flexibility, openness and a sense of humour are essential to survival at sea. Voyages aboard the *Spirit* ships foster these attributes too.

Wearing wet weather gear and safety harnesses, trainees wave-ride on the bowsprit of the **Spirit of Adventure. (Alfred Memelink)**

13

Chapter One:
Fears and Triumphs

I first sailed on the *Spirit of New Zealand* on a cold, wet Monday night at the end of June 1993. It wasn't an extended voyage, just a three-hour sail around Waitemata Harbour, departing from Marsden Wharf, where the trust's headquarters is located. Essentially, it was a chance to let members of the Supporters Club have some first-hand experience of the ship.

My first impression when I stepped aboard was that I was also stepping back in time. In the nineteenth century, the ancestors of many New Zealanders set out across the Atlantic Ocean from Britain in ships about the same size as the *Spirit* ships. There were some differences, of course. The *Spirit of New Zealand* is fitted with modern electronic gear. Less obviously to a newcomer like me, she also has a steel hull, whereas the ships that the first British settlers sailed on were predominantly wooden. But the scale was about the same. And so was the rigging.

Stephen Fisher (chairman of The Spirit of Adventure Trust) and Bill McCook (the trust's amiable chief executive) welcomed visitors on board. The ship left the wharf under motor power, but a crew of recent ex-trainees, recruited from the Voyagers Club, soon hoisted some sails. I was impressed by the confidence and apparent lack of fear with which these young people went about their tasks. Since I was lacking their wet-weather gear, however, I didn't stay on the deck chatting to them for long. Besides there were chicken wings, sausage rolls, cheese dips and pâtés waiting for the guests in the aft cabin.

After we had eaten, Stephen Fisher suggested to us that we might like to go aloft, in spite of the weather. I've always been terrified of heights, but I decided rather glumly that an ascent was probably one of the duties of authorship. I've since been told that it's better to go aloft for the first time at night, when you can't see how far you're likely to fall.

One of the Voyagers helped me clamber into a safety harness. It felt at the time as if I was being fitted for a complicated chastity belt. Harnesses, I learned, are compulsory when aloft, on the bowsprit, during night sailing, or in rough weather. I was also informed that the ropes fastened like ladder-rungs across the standing rigging are called ratlines. Nobody seems quite sure of the origin of this term, but it dates back to the fourteenth century or earlier. Inevitably, I imagined a swarm of rodents running up my trousers. I didn't really care to know either that the ropes forming the standing rigging and supporting the mast are called shrouds. I wasn't prepared to think about burial garments just yet.

The climbing was done on a 'buddy' system, with one of the Voyagers assigned to every visitor who was game enough to climb. A similar system, I later discovered, is used on special voyages arranged for people with physical disabilities. Visually impaired people, paraplegics and people with spina bifida have climbed all the way to the futtock shrouds and foretop (or platform). 'Aloft is the best place on the ship, so peaceful and quiet,' a

Above: *The* Spirit of Adventure *leaving Marsden Wharf on voyage 438.* (Tina Aarsen)

Right: *National fundraiser Vaughan Robertson, and volunteer crew member Hamish Wilson, check that this adult trainee has put her harness on correctly.*

young blind woman named Sharon Ross told the Palmerston North paper, *The Guardian*, in September 1992.

The way to climb is to take things slowly, moving only one hand or one foot at a time. The natural tendency is to cling close to the rigging with your whole body. My 'buddy' told me that it's actually safer, as well as easier, if you lean out as far as possible. I stared hard into his face. Was he kidding me? No. He knew how scared I was already. Since he had accepted me as his personal responsibility, the last thing he would want me to do was panic. I trusted him.

All the same, my hands froze on the ratlines. I didn't make it all the way to the top. I turned back after I reached the first yard (or horizontal spar), making the excuse that there were plenty of other people on the deck who still wanted a look. Since time was running out, I didn't want to be selfish by depriving them of their opportunity. Shivering, I returned to the aft cabin and gobbled everything in sight until the colour returned to my cheeks.

Another four months went by before I was next on board the *Spirit of New Zealand*. This was as a volunteer labourer to help with the annual refit. November is the month when most of the maintenance and repairs are carried out on the ships, because this is the time when high school students usually sit their examinations in New Zealand. 'Hello, I'm Steve!' a personable young man yelled to me from high in the mast. 'I need some help to get the yards down. What are you like aloft?'

Fear made me honest. 'I'm like a stranded jellyfish,' I replied. 'I'd be less use to you up there than a dead albatross. In fact, I'd be a liability to you up there.' I spent a peaceful day instead dismantling the benches on the stern.

I didn't realise at the time that I was talking to the skipper. Steve Gamble is a legendary figure in the trust, because he has gone right through the ranks, beginning as a trainee aboard the *Spirit of Adventure* on voyage 75 in 1977. He returned as a leading hand on eight subsequent voyages, then became a permanent mate in 1986 and one of the permanent masters in 1993.

To extend my experience of the ships, I went on a weekend voyage for adults aboard the *Spirit of Adventure* in February 1994. I was still green enough at the time to refer to it as a weekend cruise. Always avoided by trust employees, the word cruise gives an entirely inaccurate impression. It suggests images of wealthy passengers lazing on deckchairs in designer bathing costumes and chic sunglasses while waiters in white livery serve them martinis, mint juleps and other cocktails whenever they click their fingers. There are no passengers on the *Spirit* ships; everybody is classified as crew. Everybody is expected to help with the chores. While the *Spirits* certainly aren't convict ships or slave galleys, they aren't the *Love Boat* either.

When my boarding instructions arrived a couple of weeks in advance of the voyage around the inner Hauraki Gulf, I was dismayed to find among them a pink sheet labelled 'Useful Bends and Hitches'. Knots frighten me. Some people are dyslexic. Others have mental blocks when it comes to arithmetic or panic whenever they are confronted with diagrams or maps. I have a problem with knots. I can memorise the various formulae readily enough, so verbal quizzes do not bother me. Asked for a definition of a bowline, I can repeat by rote that it's a knot used for securing a loop that will not slip at the end of a piece of rope. I could probably tell someone else how to tie one. Yet when I'm given a piece of rope and instructed to put the theory into practice, my brain immediately turns to suet and my fingers turn to butter. I'm incapable even of tying a series of granny knots with any consistency.

Above: *All office staff crew on voyages from time to time. Here purser Judith (Pippa) Tizzard (centre) shows some trainees how to tie a bowline.*

Right: *Learning which knot not to do from crew member Frank McNamara on SONZ voyage 20.*
(Rebekah Whyte)

I looked at the pink sheet and shuddered. 'They're going to force me to tie bowlines and sheet bends and clove hitches,' I thought, 'and I'm going to scramble everything totally and look like an ass in front of a shipload of strangers. Sails worth thousands of dollars might go flying off in high winds because of my inability to secure them properly. If that happens, the crew will never forgive me. The shame of it will probably prompt me to emigrate to a distant country. A landlocked one, preferably, like Paraguay or Mali or Mongolia, where I need never sail again.

'That's if I even survive the voyage. What say we lose the mainsail through my incompetent tethering at a really crucial moment during a gale? The ship might founder in such conditions with loss of life. Even though I'm not a bad swimmer, I would probably perish, along with all the victims of my clumsy knot-tying, if the sea was very rough and the ship was a long way from shore.'

A glance through the *Instructor's Handbook* did nothing to reassure me. I found the following entry included in the syllabus outline: 'Bends & Hitches: To be able to make with eyes shut and to know the use of each. When these are completely mastered by all the watch, progress to splicing—eye, short and long splice in that order.' Not only would I be forced to tie knots, but to tie them with my eyes closed. This was calamitous news. And then there would be splicing! I hadn't even considered that gruesome possibility. What's more, there was another reference in the *Handbook* to 'Heaving lines & bollards: How to make up, bend on and throw heaving lines. How to make a monkey's fist. Turning up mooring lines on bollards. Racking seizings on bollards.'

It might as well have been written in Sanskrit or ancient Egyptian hieroglyphics for all the sense it made to me. What on earth was a heaving line? A queue to chunder over the side of the ship, perhaps? Were bollards the nautical equivalent of what ordinary folk referred to as bollocks? And why on earth would anybody, except a monkey, want to make a monkey's fist?

Further scrutiny of the *Handbook* bred further anxieties. I have never had any sense of direction. How would I get on with compasses and navigation? The text referred to mysterious things I had never even heard of—lubber lines and azimuth rings. The dictionary told me that an azimuth is 'the angular distance from a north or south point of the horizon to the intersection with the horizon of a vertical circle passing through a celestial body'. Frankly, I didn't understand this. It was too hard for me. My eyes just swam uncomprehendingly over the definition.

Fastening the head lashings of the Spirit of New Zealand's *mainsail with reef knots and sewing them for extra security. Stephen Fisher, chairman of The Spirit of Adventure Trust, is on the right.* (Tessa Duder)

'I'm going to get everything wrong,' I fretted. 'I'm going to disgrace myself by trying to heave a lubber line at a bollard. I'll probably make a monkey's fist out of my azimuth ring.'

My fears were irrational, exaggerated, downright silly, yet still potent. The masters, mates and watch leaders don't expect trainees to know much when they first step aboard. They certainly didn't expect me to know about azimuths. Or to do any splicing. One of the mates explained to me, when I asked, that a bollard is just the nautical name for any short post to which ropes are secured.

The permanent crew are trained to be meticulous in all matters of safety. Apart from a few minor bruises, cuts and broken bones and teeth, there has never been a serious accident aboard either of the *Spirit* ships. The officers would never let an important knot tied by a nervous-looking novice go unchecked. No sail is reliant on just a single knot anyway. Nor are the ships ever reliant on a single sail or a single trainee. If need be, they can easily switch to motor power. They are fully equipped with life rafts and life jackets, but during the 21 years that The Spirit of Adventure Trust has been in operation these have never needed to be used in earnest. I knew all these facts, but I still worried. I let my imagination run wild until I was fretting absurdly about possible loss of life, but what I was really anxious about was loss of face. I was afraid of being put in a position where my weaknesses would be exposed in front of others. I didn't want to be embarrassed.

I thought again about the term 'psychological development'. What do we mean when we refer to people 'developing', as if they were photographs? I suspect that what we're really talking about is the gradual conquest of fears, anxieties, mental blocks and sources of panic. Different things scare different people. I'm afraid of making a fool of myself whenever I'm handed a piece of rope and told to tie a knot in it. Or whenever I'm handed a map and expected to make sense of it. Or whenever I have to climb more than a couple of metres off the ground.

The *Spirit of Adventure*'s masts are about 25 metres high (to be precise, the foremast is 24.34 metres, and the main mast is 25.53 metres). Although

Does author Iain Sharp, pictured aboard the **Spirit of Adventure** *during a weekend voyage in February 1994, really know what he's doing with this sheet?* (John Duder)

Almost all trainees are nervous at first about going aloft, but most overcome their fear after a few days.

it's not mandatory, almost all the trainees on ten-day voyages end up climbing them. Partly this is a matter of peer pressure, but it's also an insistent kind of challenge from within. On weekend trips it's easy to wriggle out of ever going aloft, but you feel like a terrible wimp if you don't even try.

I had done a bit of homework before the weekend voyage. I knew that Santa Claus had once climbed the main mast. In October 1974 the *Spirit of Adventure* was used in a television advertisement for Choysa tea. Part of this included Santa swinging down from the mast with a sackload of booty, which included the tea. 'If Santa can do it,' I thought, 'so can I.' This wasn't particularly logical of me, since there are many things that Mr Claus can do that I obviously can't.

I took it in stages. What I had been told was true. Climbing the mast is actually more difficult in daylight when you can see exactly what it is you have to do. First, I put on a harness and just stood on the deck for a while gazing skywards before removing the harness again. A little later, I had another go and got as far this time as actually putting my hands on the ratlines.

Then, after a while, I managed to climb gingerly up the ratlines a little way and come back down again. I didn't succeed in climbing all the way to the top during my first weekend voyage, but eventually I reached as far as the futtocks halfway up the foremast. I felt like a hero, for I had overcome, at least partly, my lifelong acrophobia. The real value of sail training comes from small victories of this kind.

Snoring, I must confess, was another of my anxieties. The trainees on the *Spirit* ships sleep in hammock-style bunks. For the sake of propriety, there are separate male and female quarters, but there are not separate cabins. You sleep surrounded by vertical, horizontal and diagonal neighbours. If you snore, you can easily keep half the ship awake. I'm the sort of heavy sleeper who can snooze uninterrupted during a brass band parade or a hurricane, so I had no fears at all about other people depriving me of my rest. On the other hand, I have been informed in the past, somewhat irately, that I snore. 'Oh heavens,' I thought, 'I could bend over backwards being polite and helpful to everybody all day and still end up the least popular person aboard because of the involuntary racket I make at night. It's just as well this is only a weekend sail. On a longer journey, snoring could become a justifiable cause for homicide.'

I was so tense about giving inadvertent nocturnal offence to the people around me that it took me a couple of hours to fall asleep my first night aboard the *Spirit of Adventure*. They were instructive hours, though, for as I lay awake listening I learned that plenty of other folk snore too. Compared with some of the vigorous gargles, snorts and buzzsaw impersonations I could hear, I probably wasn't such a night-time monster after all. I felt grateful for the reassurance.

Because of the limited shower facilities on the ships and the need to conserve water, the young people on ten-day voyages are expected to take a daily 6 a.m. dip in the ocean, even in winter, for purposes of hygiene as well as character building. Adult weekenders are treated more gently. They're invited to have a pre-breakfast swim, but they can decline if they wish.

By and large I'm an early riser and I have swum in the sea since I was a small boy. I wouldn't dare to compare myself as a swimmer with Tessa Duder, who won a silver medal for the women's 110-yard butterfly at the 1958 Empire Games in Cardiff, but I can stay afloat. So, when I first heard ex-trainees speak with dread of the morning splash, I tended to laugh because I thought they were just objecting to such a cold start to the day. It took

Left: *Camaraderie in the* Spirit of New Zealand*'s sleeping quarters.*

Below: *Supervised by the cook, Derryn Wilson, a group of trainees helps store provisions in the* Spirit of New Zealand *galley.* (Tessa Duder)

me a while to realise that for some of them the fear was more profound. There's a requirement that every trainee is capable of swimming 100 metres before joining the programme, but many youngsters have never swum in the ocean out of their depth with no land in sight. They're used to the safety of pools and beaches.

There's nothing young people hate more than an accusation of immaturity especially if it comes from their peers. For this reason, they're generally reluctant to discuss the ways in which they're metaphorically out of their depth during the ten-day voyages. For many of them, this is the first time they have been away from family and friends for any extended period. The trainees on any given voyage are strangers to one another when they embark. They come from different schools, different parts of the country and different social backgrounds.

It's always frightening at first to join a group of strangers. Even as a 40-year-old, going away for only a weekend, I felt a little apprehensive as I stepped aboard the *Spirit of Adventure*. 'What if I don't like these people?' I wondered. 'What if they don't like me?' But these flashes of doubt were very mild compared with the agonies I used to go through as a shy and awkward adolescent. The discovery that they're acceptable human beings who can make friends is the most important aspect of the voyages for many trainees.

Some of the young trainees come from rather sheltered backgrounds. Dawn McIntyre, a volunteer cook on several ten-day voyages, told me about one lad who was assigned to help her with the dishes. He looked around the galley with growing alarm. He looked left and right, up and down, fore and aft, under the tables and even into the cupboards. 'B . . . b . . . but where's the dishwashing machine?' he finally cried in panic.

Volunteer watch leader Lyn Goldsworthy told me about another young trainee who was asked to swab down the decks at the end of the ten-day voyage. It was clear from his lackadaisical sweeping that he had rarely, if ever, held a brush before. 'I think you need a bit more elbow grease there!' Lyn yelled to him. He dropped what he was doing and began to search the ship for a can of this hitherto unheard-of lubricant.

On the last day of their ten-day voyages, the trainees are expected to sail the ship by themselves. Crew members step in only in emergencies. The proper aim of any educative process is to render the teacher redundant. Of course, after less than a fortnight at sea, the teenagers still have a long way to go before they become master mariners. But, to return to an earlier point, the aim is not to produce future skippers, it's to help people develop greater confidence in themselves and their attitudes on life.

The challenges involved are a little different for every person who comes on board. I have no fear of the ocean, but I was thrilled with myself for climbing as high as the futtocks. Conversely, there were some folk on my weekend voyage who seemed to be part monkey and dangled for hours from the highest parts of the mast with an expression of sheer bliss, yet they had to steel themselves to overcome their fear of swimming in the open sea. A natural loner and nighthawk might enjoy the 3 a.m. watch but be intimidated by communal meals and sleeping arrangements. A natural chatterbox who likes at least eight hours of uninterrupted sleep per night will have the reverse problem. Depending on your family circumstances, a big pile of dishes might seem like a daily task not worth commenting on (just as you wouldn't bother commenting on having to brush your teeth), or it could appear to be a major calamity. There are those who can simultaneously tie a figure eight with their left hand while executing a round turn and two half-hitches with their right. But for me even a reef knot is a major victory.

Chapter Two:
Launching an Idea

If all the people who have been involved with the *Spirit of Adventure* and the *Spirit of New Zealand* over the last 21 years—all the board members, ship builders, administrative staff, fund-raisers, school principals, full-time crew members, volunteers and trainees—were gathered together in one place, there would be enough folk not only to fill a sports stadium but to populate a small town. Teamwork has always been the essence of the *Spirit* project. No matter how fit and ingenious you are, if you want to take a 33-metre topsail schooner or a 45-metre barquentine on a ten-day voyage, you will soon need help. Nobody can manage such an undertaking single-handedly. It's a big co-operative venture.

Nevertheless, when outlining the history of The Spirit of Adventure Trust, it makes sense to narrow the focus at first to one dynamic personality: Auckland businessman Lou Fisher (1913–77). Although he was always ready to acknowledge the help he had from others, the trust can properly be described as Lou Fisher's brainchild. It would not exist without his initial injection of time, money and enthusiasm.

The Fisher family has been prominent in New Zealand industry since the 1930s. Like his older brother Woolf (the co-founder of Fisher and Paykel), his younger brother Gus, and his three sisters, Midge, Floss and Pearl, Lou was a person of huge energy, capable of turning his agile mind to many different kinds of endeavour.

He began his business career in the fashion industry, before serving overseas in the Second World War. Later he ran a town supply dairy farm, manufactured rotary mowers and eventually diversified into building materials,

Above: *Auckland businessman Lou Fisher (1913–77) was the driving force and principal benefactor behind The Spirit of Adventure Trust in its early years.* (The Fisher family)

Opposite: *The foredeck of the* Spirit of Adventure *viewed from aloft.* (Alfred Memelink)

25

including Decramastic roofing tiles, Fisher windows and Ranchslider doors.

He believed that successful men like himself ought to make worthwhile contributions to the communities in which they lived. Thus he was a linchpin in numerous philanthropic organisations, including Rotary, the World Wildlife Fund, the Auckland Sheltered Workshop and the Bethells Beach Lifesaving Club. Without fanfare, he provided the finance to build tennis courts in the Pakuranga area and he was the main mover behind the construction of the Panmure Young Citizens Centre, which, in spite of its name, now provides facilities for people of all ages. With his wife, Iris, he often let local groups use the spacious grounds of his house beside Tamaki Estuary for social and fund-raising activities.

Although his commercial and humanitarian interests necessarily absorbed much of his time, he was also a keen sportsman. Riding was his first passion. He regularly participated in the Pakuranga Hunt and for many years he also owned and bred racehorses. In the late 1950s his champion filly Yahabeebe was one of the best sprinters in New Zealand.

He discovered the joys and challenges of sailing comparatively late in life. He was 45 before he purchased his first yacht. But he did not start out on a small scale, like most Aucklanders, with a trailer sailer. Built in England at the turn of the century, *Imatra* was a magnificent 33-metre ketch with mahogany and walnut panelling, velvet cushions, red carpets and even a copper bath in the sumptuous living quarters below deck. It was typical of Lou to want to share this treasure—and not just with his business colleagues. When he took her on weekend trips from Auckland to Kawau Island (a distance of about 25 nautical miles), his crew usually consisted of his young son Stephen (just ten years old when the trips began) and a large contingent of Stephen's school mates. The guiding philosophy seems to have been the more the merrier. 'Once we took a cub pack, 40 strong,' Stephen recalls. Sometimes Lou's three daughters—Janet, Susan and Frances—and their friends would come along too.

Although fun was the main priority on these family excursions, youth development was a topic that interested Lou and he noticed how the gradual mastering of sailing techniques had a beneficial effect on the youngsters aboard *Imatra*, improving their perseverance, concentration, comradeship and self-confidence. Although more than a decade went by before he committed himself to financing a sail training ship, the seed of the idea was planted in his mind during the Kawau trips in the late 1950s and early 1960s.

Sail training has a long history. When James Cook sailed the *Endeavour* into New Zealand waters in July 1769, he was 40 years old and arguably the most experienced mariner in the world, since none of his contemporaries could match his first-hand knowledge of such vast tracts of ocean. Yet even Cook had been a raw trainee once. Although he grew up near the Yorkshire port of Whitby, at the mouth of the River Esk, he did not come from a seafaring family. The son of a farmhand, he began his working life as a haberdasher's apprentice. He was 18 when he joined a Whitby-based shipping company which operated trading barques across the North Sea. He must have approached his first maritime voyage with the same nervous excitement and sense of anxiety about how well he would measure up as young people today aboard the *Spirit* ships.

The naval history of New Zealand does not begin with Cook, however. Mention must be made not only of the brilliant Dutch explorer Abel Tasman a century earlier but also of the great navigational skills of the Maori people. Sail training might not be the appropriate term, since Maori vessels were propelled as much by paddles as by sails, but hundreds of years before the arrival of the first Europeans in these islands canoecraft was already an essential component in the education of every Maori youth.

Looked at from a broad perspective, the concept of sail training is almost as old as civilisation itself. Even in ancient times, cities were built close to natural harbours and wind-assisted boats were used as a means of transport. Five thousand years ago, young Egyptians must have been instructed in the rudiments of rigging, luffing, tacking and navigation by more experienced sailors. Every navy since then has needed to devise some kind of educative system whereby greenhorns can eventually become proficient mariners. The shapes of masts and sails varied over the centuries, as did the reliance on subsidiary oar power, but the basic lore absorbed by budding seamen remained pretty much the same from the heyday of the Phoenicians in the first millennium BC until the advent of steamships in the 1820s. Nor did steam take over immediately. Sailing ships were still a common sight in the Pacific and Atlantic in the first decades of the twentieth century.

In January 1990, as part of New Zealand's sesquicentennial celebrations, the Spirit *ships took part in a tall ships race at Russell in the Bay of Islands. From left to right: the* Breeze *(New Zealand), the* Spirit of Adventure, *the* R. Tucker Thompson *(New Zealand), the* Young Endeavour *(Australia), and the* Tradewind *(New Zealand). Also present, but not shown, were the* Spirit of New Zealand *and the* Soren Larsen *(UK).* **(Nathan Bilow)**

Lou Fisher with trainees on an early voyage aboard the Spirit of Adventure.

(Auckland Star)

In New Zealand the Union Steamship Company trained cadets on its three-masted iron barque *Dartford* until 1912. From 1905 to 1921, the New Zealand Government used the barquentine *Amokura*, formerly HMS *Sparrow*, to train boys aged between 12 and 15 for the merchant service and the Royal Navy. As late as 1949, the four-masted barque *Pamir* still plied New Zealand waters and future harbourmasters, pilots and surveyors first learned their seamanship as young apprentices aboard her.

Lou Fisher's intentions in the early 1970s, though, were not quite identical with those of ancient chiefs or the Royal New Zealand Navy. He was not trying to produce a corps of professional sailors. His focus was on psychological development rather than vocational training. The building of stalwart characters mattered much more to him than the tying of meticulous knots. He hoped to foster qualities of self-reliance, initiative, fortitude and co-operation in young minds. However, it's important not to give a false impression of the man by making him appear too serious or loftily Victorian in his outlook. Sailing was, above all, fun for Lou and he wanted others to share his pleasure. A succinct summary of his aims can be found in the minutes of the first meeting of the trust board he set up in 1972. The reason for building a sail training ship was to help young people 'develop a potential for leadership, learn to live together, develop a knowledge of ships and the sea and enjoy themselves'.

Lou was a district chairman of the Sea Scouts, the maritime sub-section of the scouting movement established by Warington Baden-Powell (Robert's more nautically inclined younger brother) in 1910. The New Zealand branches of the Sea Scouts generally worked with small yachts and dinghies (and stretched their finances to include boat ownership), but nevertheless they provided an antecedent for Fisher's belief in the link between good seamanship and good citizenship. He was also aware of the success of sail training organisations in other parts of the world, particularly Britain.

After the Second World War, when large sailing ships seemed likely to die out completely, old sailors around the globe, who had learned their craft aboard schooners, barques and ketches, began to protest that there were lessons learned through toiling with masts and rigging which could not be duplicated elsewhere. Surely lore that had been a valuable part of human experience for centuries was worth rescuing from oblivion? Some navies heeded the plea and retained an old-fashioned vessel or two specifically for the training of cadets. Interest in the idea extended beyond the armed forces, however. In the 1950s, private trusts were formed in many parts of the world either to restore venerable craft from the past or to construct new sailing ships so that young people could benefit from the challenge of an ocean voyage under canvas.

Driven by the enthusiasm of a London solicitor, Bernard Morgan, whose initial ambition was to organise a race from Torbay, in southwest England, across the Bay of Biscay to Lisbon for the last of the world's great square-riggers, Britain's Sail Training Association was founded in 1956. For nearly a decade they survived without a ship of their own. Then in the mid-60s they raised sufficient funds to build a pair of large topsail schooners: *Sir Winston Churchill*, launched in 1966 and *Malcolm Miller* (named after the son of one of the principal benefactors, Sir James Miller, a former Lord Mayor of London), which was launched in 1968. Thereafter, instead of racing, the association's primary business was to arrange sea-going adventures, usually of a fortnight's duration, for young people aged between 15 and 20.

Lou watched the progress of these British schooners with great interest. By 1970 he had decided to devote time and energy to creating a similar scheme in New Zealand. There were many questions to resolve, however. What kind of ship would be the most suitable for local conditions? How many trainees should she carry at a time? How long should a typical voyage be? How should the trainees be selected? Would this be just an Auckland-based venture or a national one? How would the project be funded? How much should the trainees be asked to pay for a voyage? How many full-time crew members were needed?

To help work out the details, Lou sought advice from seafaring friends, business colleagues and educationalists. Gradually he assembled a group of trustees who met for the first time in July 1972. With Lou Fisher as chairman, the founding members of the board were Rear Admiral Laurie Carr, John Brooke (an Auckland yacht designer whose task it was to draw up the plans for the proposed training ship), Peter Mulgrew (a renowned yachtsman, mountaineer and polar explorer), Barry Thompson (a master mariner who had served with the British Merchant Service and the Royal New Zealand Navy Volunteer Reserve), Colin Maiden (vice-chancellor of the University of Auckland), John McKenzie (a lawyer and keen yachtsman), Simon Caughey (an energetic young businessman) and Stephen Fisher (already an accomplished yachtsman at the age of 24). Although the

The Spirit of Adventure *at Te Kouma Harbour, Coromandel Peninsula.* (Alfred Memelink)

composition of the board has changed considerably over the years, the aim has always been to maintain the original blend of business and sailing expertise and an element of those who shared Lou Fisher's original aims.

As Lou Fisher's vision of the sail-training programme grew, so did the ship's dimensions. When he first approached his old friend John Brooke in 1971 with the idea of designing a vessel to take young people on ocean adventures, what Lou had in mind was a 75-foot (22.86-metre) ketch, but the length eventually increased to 85 feet (25.9 metres), then 90 feet (27.44 metres), and he began to think in terms of a proper ship rather than just a big yacht. Brooke grumbled about how naval architecture is a very tricky procedure and changes cannot be effected in a matter of minutes just by rubbing out a few lines here and there, but fortunately he was a patient man.

He was versatile too, much like Lou. Although he was a superb yacht designer, this had not been his primary profession throughout his working life. Born in Cheltenham, Auckland, in 1907, he taught at Seddon Technical College until the Second World War, then moved to Wellington to work on designing tools and gauges for munitions at the Dominion Physical laboratories, a forerunner of the Department of Scientific and Industrial Research (DSIR). After the war, he became director of the Auckland industrial development division of DSIR for the next 25 years. He had just resigned from this position when he began work on the *Spirit of Adventure*.

Founder Lou Fisher (centre), the first master for the trust, Pony Moore (far left), and Rear Admiral Laurie Carr (right), one of the founding trustees, during the 'shake-down' voyage on board the Spirit of Adventure, *December–January 1973–74.*

At first the ketch was to have a wooden hull, but as the size expanded steel became the more economic option. The original sail design followed conventional ketch rigging. Then Barry Thompson returned from a visit to the Sail Training Association in England convinced that the British decision to incorporate some square rig in their training ships made good sense. A square sail needs to be supported by a series of horizontal spars, known as yards, as well as a mast. Since the essence of the training scheme was to present young people with a worthwhile challenge, why not give them the opportunity to climb aloft and dangle from a yardarm in a howling gale? Fisher was soon persuaded that ketch rigging would be unsatisfyingly easy and Brooke was instructed to amend his drawings yet again.

By the time the Auckland boatbuilding firm Vos & Brijs (located then as now at 14 Hamer Street, St Mary's Bay) began construction in May 1972, the ship bore very little resemblance to Brooke's initial design.

Meanwhile the trust board decided that trainees should consist mainly of adolescents aged between 15 and 19 and selected with the help of school principals throughout New Zealand. Schools would be encouraged to consider less obvious candidates as well as their finest and fittest pupils (the duxes, head prefects and sports captains). A week was regarded as the absolute minimum time for a programme in which trainees would reap real benefits rather than just coming along for a short holiday cruise. Two weeks would have been ideal. Ten-day voyages were the eventual compromise, since these allowed room every month for maintenance and repairs. A few years later, weekend sailings were added for adults who would pay the full fee, thereby generating funds by which the young trainees could have their voyage fees subsidised.

Because they were keen to present themselves as a national rather than regional organisation and to provide an equal opportunity for all, the board proposed to pay the long-distance travel expenses of trainees from other districts who were required to make their way to Auckland to join the ship.

The stipulation that the training ship should operate within the Auckland region, confined essentially to the inner Hauraki Gulf, had come from the Marine Division of the Ministry of Transport. It had been more than half a century since the ministry's surveyors last had to consider the whys and wherefores of a large sailing ship and they had never

The bow of the **Spirit of Adventure**, *showing one of the wooden dolphin ornaments presented by the Voyagers Club in 1984 and subsequently lost at sea.* (John Klingenberg)

before encountered trainees who were not attached to the navy. Thus they preferred to be cautious. Once the scheme proved successful, permission was granted for the ship to journey to other New Zealand ports by special voyage permit and, in more recent times, by being certified as a coastal ship.

The name *Spirit of Adventure*, an excellent distillation of the guiding philosophy behind the scheme, was Lou Fisher's suggestion, but there had been considerable agonising before he thought of it out of the blue one Sunday morning over breakfast with his wife Iris. The *Adventure* was the name of the ship which accompanied James Cook's *Resolution* on the great English navigator's second voyage of Pacific exploration in the 1770s, but the connection, though pleasing, was not deliberate.

The cost of the *Spirit of Adventure* has never been disclosed by the Fisher family. It has been estimated at around $300,000 (or the equivalent of $5 million in contemporary currency), but the full price of construction is difficult to calculate because right from the start there were well-wishers who were prepared to donate services and materials. The Auckland Harbour Board provided free berthing and office space on Marsden Wharf. Without this accommodation, the project might never have gone ahead.

The *Spirit of Adventure* carries 24 trainees and a crew of nine (master, mates, watch officers, engineer and cook) plus a leading hand and a cadet. From early days female trainees have been as welcome as male, although the original nature of the accommodation area (since modified) precluded the possibility of integrated voyages. Lou Fisher also wanted trainees to come from all social classes. Ideally, he would have liked the charge per trainee to have been only $30 for a ten-day voyage, but this proved an unrealistic target. Still, the fee was just $50 per head for the first voyage around the islands of the Hauraki Gulf from 22 January to 1 February 1974. Since then charges have risen steadily in keeping with inflation, with the trainees paying about two-thirds of the actual cost of running the programme. Fund-raising continues to be of crucial concern to the trust board.

In spite of dour predictions early on that seasick young sailors were bound to plummet to their deaths from the swaying yardarms, there has never been a serious accident aboard either of the *Spirit* ships. Mishaps of any kind have been remarkably few, given the youthful personnel. The *Spirit of Adventure* did, however, get off to a rather shaky start. One of the most embarrassing moments in her 21-year career took place during the launching.

Saturday, 8 December 1973 was a beautifully sunny day. Proud members of the trust board and their families assembled in the early evening at the Vos & Brijs yard in Hamer Street. At 5.15 p.m. Susan Fisher, Lou's 21-year-old daughter, successfully smashed a champagne bottle across the bow in the time-honoured way, but the *Spirit* refused to budge. She had to be eased down the slipway with jacks. Once she began to move, however, she was unstoppable. She sped down the rails at an unseemly angle, bent her rudder as she bounced off the bottom even though it was high tide and then collided with a hapless spectator's keeler. In the two decades since then she has never been so ill-behaved.

For the last 21 years, the *Spirit of Adventure* has consistently lived up to the promise envisaged by Lou Fisher. 'We are a maritime nation and our youth can learn much from the sea,' he said in his address to the crowd assembled at St Mary's Bay for the launching. 'It is important that a training voyage on this vessel is always within reach for a young New Zealander, no matter where he or she may live, and regardless of social background.'

33

Chapter Three:
The Second Ship

When the *Spirit of Adventure* embarked on her first ten-day voyage in January 1974, she was not yet fully rigged. It was not until her tenth voyage, four months later, that the yards for the square sails were fitted and not until the fourteenth voyage, in September 1974, that the ship first appeared under full sail. Inevitably, some technical problems had to be resolved in the early days. The original aluminium foremast, for instance, was too light. It bent ominously whenever the *Spirit* reached speeds of ten knots or more. Within a few months, it was replaced by a heavier mast of spiral-welded steel.

Although they were all experienced sailors, the first master, Pony More (who had helped supervise the *Spirit of Adventure*'s construction) and the members of the crew needed time to adapt to the new ship. A full-sized sailing ship is different from a large yacht in the way the group of sails interact and in the development of the power necessary to get the best out of a large sailing ship, particularly going to windward. Besides, nobody had done this before in New Zealand; they needed to become good students as well as good sailors. On the inaugural ten-day voyage, the officers had as much to learn as the trainees. It's hardly surprising that they made a few gaffes, such as hoisting one of the sails (the upper fisherman) upside down and nearly putting the boom through the deck when the mainsail was first dropped. Everybody learned quickly, however, and there were no serious mishaps or delays between voyages.

In Europe, it's not uncommon for sail training ships to be out of action for

Even in rough weather, the trainees can still have a good time — the rougher the better for some of them!

(Alfred Memelink)

Previous page: *The* Spirit of New Zealand *in Oriental Bay, Wellington.* (Alfred Memelink)

The Spirit of Adventure ***with a squall approaching.*** (Cliff Hawkins)

as much as a third of the year because winter conditions are too harsh for young novices to cope with. Because of New Zealand's comparatively mild climate, the *Spirit of Adventure* has always sailed all the year round. But describing the local weather as temperate in comparison with northern Europe is not the same as saying it's invariably placid. New Zealand trainees have sometimes been obliged to withstand howling gales.

Voyage 25 (a shipload of teenage girls) struck the tail end of Cyclone Alison when returning to Auckland from the Coromandel Peninsula in March 1975. The girls impressed with their nonchalance (at least after the event). 'It was my first time out on a yacht,' fifth-former Jill Cordes told weekly Auckland newspaper, the *Eight O'Clock,* 'and it was terrific. It was really rough and a few of us were seasick, but everyone enjoyed it, although the captain told us later he was a bit worried.'

Voyage 70, in January 1977, had to be rescued at 3 a.m. by the Tauranga Harbour tug after the *Spirit*'s propeller was fouled by a small yacht's anchor rope at Mayor Island. It had been calm when the ship anchored in South-East Bay, but by 11 p.m. a heavy storm set in. All the small craft in the bay started to drag their anchors and a small yacht drifted under the *Spirit*'s stern. The master at the time, Stan Hulford, said, 'We had to let our anchor go and the ship drifted close to the shore. At one stage during the night I assembled the girls on the quarterdeck wearing their life jackets and explained that we were in a tricky situation.' At 12.35 a.m. he radioed the Bay of Plenty Harbour Board for assistance. A Harbour Board diver later removed about nine metres of line and chain from the propeller.

Fred Hansen, who became a master with the trust in 1976, recalls an occasion, returning from the Bay of Islands, when the *Spirit of Adventure* 'was thrown off the top of a wave and knocked on her beam ends so that the lower yard touched the water. We blew out four sails. Lost a life raft too.'

Bad weather has never kept the ships out of commission for long, though, and they have always achieved their programmes. The only time of the year when the ships don't sail for more than a day or two is during November. Usually a fine spring month in New Zealand, November has been set side for maintenance and refitting since 1975.

During their first decade, The Spirit of Adventure Trust greatly expanded their zone of operations. Right from the start, the trainees were selected from every part of the country, but the voyages themselves were initially confined to Auckland's waters. Then in February 1976 a new certificate of survey permitted the ship to sail about half the length of the North Island from North Cape (often mistaken for New Zealand's northernmost point) to East Cape (the easternmost promontory of the North Island). The following month the *Spirit* called for the first time at the northern port of Whangarei. In 1977 she visited the port of Tauranga and participated in the Waitangi Day celebrations in the Bay of Islands. By 1979 the *Spirit* had been granted the right to travel the full length of the country. She embarked on her first major southern cruise in March of that year, visiting Gisborne and Wellington, crossing Cook Strait, calling at Picton and Anakiwa (the site of New Zealand's Outward Bound School, at the head of Queen Charlotte Sound, Marlborough), and then returning to Auckland via Napier and Tauranga. She visited the Canterbury ports of Akaroa (84 kilometres southeast of Christchurch) and Lyttelton (about 12 kilometres east of Christchurch's Cathedral Square) for the first time in March 1980 and the following year she ventured even further south to Timaru, Dunedin, Bluff and Oban (the main port and chief settlement on Stewart Island, 35 kilometres south by boat across Foveaux Strait from Bluff). A complete circumnavigation of New Zealand was undertaken between December 1983 and May 1984.

The trainees on the first few voyages were boys aged from 15 to 17, but the intention from the beginning was for the *Spirit* experience to be available to both sexes. The first ten-day voyage for girls embarked on 11 June 1974, and thereafter the number of trainees selected from each sex has been just about equal, although in the early years the expeditions were usually segregated. (A mixed weekend voyage for 15 Venturer Scouts and 12 Ranger Guides from the Howick-Pakuranga area in September 1975 was an early exception to the general rule.)

The trustees were also keen to include young people with physical disabilities. A day sail from Auckland to Rakino Island was arranged for 15 boys from the Kelston School for the Deaf on 21 December 1974. Since then the general policy has been to integrate teenagers with mild physical disabilities into the ordinary programme and to arrange special voyages for more severely disabled young people who require one-to-one attention. Thirteen visually impaired youngsters from Homai College, the Blind Foundation and Manurewa

Special voyages are arranged for young people with disabilities who are partnered by able-bodied 'buddies'. Watched by his buddy, Jeremy Takacs, and voyage organiser, Joyce Lavender, trainee Jeremy Persen learns the ropes aboard the Spirit of New Zealand.

A special harness helps Daniel Carswell from Feilding, who has cerebral palsy, get a taste of the water.

Second mate Deanna Douglas helps Teresa Munro, who is paralysed on her left side, climb aloft.

Intermediate School (all in South Auckland) were taken for a day sail around the inner Hauraki Gulf in October 1983. There have been many longer voyages for the physically disabled since that time, involving a 'buddy' system in which each disabled person is assisted throughout the journey by an able-bodied Voyager.

Although young people in their mid-teens have always been the principal focus of the *Spirit* project, voyages for other age groups were established early on. Voyage 16, in October 1974, carried a complement of naval apprentices aged between 17 and 21, and voyage 17 was crewed by Sea Scouts aged between 11 and 15. The smaller boys had trouble coping with the winches in heavy weather, but they are still remembered fondly by *Spirit* staff today for their pluck and fortitude on the second-to-last day of the expedition, when the ship encountered northeasterlies gusting up to 45 knots and heeled over to a terrifying 44 degrees, thereby stalling the motor.

A second Sea Scout voyage in September 1977 was similarly plagued by bad weather. It was a weekend voyage. The storm occurred on the Saturday, just after a practice of man-overboard and abandon-ship drills. The decks were awash. They made it into Man of War Bay on Waiheke Island, where they stayed the night until the storm died down.

The oldest ever trainee was Martin Cook, born on 25 March 1889, who took part in a Monday night training voyage under the command of his grandson Brian Whiteman in October 1988. Mr Cook, whose home was at Whitley Bay on the northeast coast of England, decided to travel to New Zealand to visit Brian. While in New Zealand, as well as serving his turn at the wheel of the *Spirit of Adventure*, he went on a jet boat trip up to the Huka Falls along the Waikato River.

As for as the youngest trainees, I have seen a newspaper photograph of 15-month-old Karen Goodwin taking the wheel during an open day aboard the *Spirit of Adventure* in April 1979 when the ship was visiting the Port of Tauranga. But possibly Karen can't be counted as a proper trainee, since she was held by her mother at the time. Ben Fisher, son of Stephen and Virginia Fisher, was even younger—a mere six weeks old—when he was first taken on a day sail with other guests and trainees in Wellington Harbour.

Trustee Barry Thompson suggested the idea of weekend voyages for adults early in 1976. He considered it wasteful for the *Spirit of Adventure* to sit unused alongside Marsden Wharf for two weekends every month between the scheduled ten-day voyages. During the first year of operation, the trust's financial deficit was $15,000 and for 1975 it was $25,000, even after a special one-off grant of $8500 from the Ministry of Recreation and Sport. As running costs continued to rise, the trust had to look at new ways of generating income. It wasn't unreasonable to ask adults to pay in full, thus providing some extra money to help subsidise school-aged trainees on longer voyages. Not that there was any expectation of raising enough capital from the weekenders to balance the books, even if the ship was operated by volunteer crew. Raffles and other forms of fund-raising remained crucial for the *Spirit*'s continued existence. Though the motivation behind weekend voyages was partly financial, they served a social purpose which was always perceived as being as important as the monetary gain. They were a way of letting supporters and well-wishers sample life aboard the *Spirit* at first hand. The first adult weekender took place from 12 to 14 March 1975. They have been a regular part of the trust's operation ever since.

Lou Fisher seldom had the opportunity to sail on the *Spirit*, but by the time of his death in May 1977 more than 2000 young trainees had been on ten-day voyages. Lou's will vested ownership of the ship in the trust board.

His commitment had been absolute. With the operation running at an annual deficit of

$18,000, he told the *New Zealand Herald* in December 1976, 'We have accepted responsibility for the scheme and we are doing something about it. It just means we will have to work a little harder. We would explore all possible angles before considering raising the fees. Obviously we would like life to be a little easier, but we know it is not going to be. And we are determined to carry on.'

The number of people who could claim a connection with the *Spirit of Adventure* continued to grow steadily. When the Supporters Club was launched in September 1974 by Sir Dove-Myer Robinson (the long-serving Mayor of Auckland who was at the height of his popularity in the 1970s), 60 people attended the first public meeting, but by the end of that year the club boasted 400 members. At the end of 1977 membership was up to 1000 and by the start of the 1980s it was around 2000. The subscription at first was only $5 a year.

The growth of the Voyagers Club for former trainees was just as rapid. Early in 1975, Ron Bird, the *Spirit*'s first permanent engineer and a tireless enthusiast for all *Spirit*-related activities, produced a humble one-sheet newsletter for ex-trainees called *The Voyager*. A

Too many chiefs and not enough Indians? On voyage 458SP, the Spirit of Adventure *was crewed entirely by captains during a special masters' training voyage. Back row, left to right: Steve Gamble, Andrew Lidgard, Bill Curry, Ken Bedford, Graeme Darroch (engineer); middle row: Jennifer Roberts, Rick Hunter, Peter Petherbridge, Geoff Rowarth, Pony More, Neil Rowarth, Alan Wallis; front row: Paul Leppington, Barry Thompson, Hugh Munro, Roy Swan, Con Thode, Ian Rankin.*

reunion ball was held on Saturday, 14 August 1976, in the West End Rowing Club Reception Lounge, 7 p.m. to midnight, dress semi-formal. Two years later, the Voyagers Club was a national organisation with branches throughout the country, holding frequent social gatherings, balls, reunions and fund-raising drives. By the end of 1981, nearly 5000 trainees had sailed on the *Spirit* and no-one could deny that the scheme was a huge success. The trustees began to discuss the possibility of selling the *Spirit of Adventure* in order to fund the building of a larger ship which would better meet the demand from schools and other institutions around New Zealand.

The decision to keep the existing ship in a state of good repair and build a larger vessel as well came almost as a royal command. When visiting New Zealand in October 1981, H.R.H. The Prince Philip, Duke of Edinburgh, who had taken a lively interest in sail training in Britain since the 1950s, was keen to inspect the *Spirit of Adventure*. While chatting with Stephen Fisher (who had become chairman of the trust board on the death of his father) and Iris Fisher (Lou's widow) in the great cabin, he learned of the plan afoot to replace the ship with a bigger vessel. 'Be damned if you're going to sell her,' Prince Philip announced with his characteristic forthrightness. 'You're going to operate two.' Fund-raising for a second ship began soon after.

Stephen Fisher told the *Auckland Star* in July 1982, 'The reason for building a second boat, the *Spirit of New Zealand*, is to give more young New Zealanders a spell at sea. We realise the ideal training period is ten days. We don't want to shorten it. We can't take any additional youngsters because the ship is already operating throughout the year. We considered whether to go for a sister ship, to replace with a bigger vessel or to purchase an existing vessel. The most economic choice appears to be to build a bigger ship. Depending on the campaign we will decide whether we can continue to run both vessels.'

There was no real argument this time about the kind of ship required. Square sails, everyone agreed, were a must. The architects, Don Brooke and Ted Ewbank, took their cue from a historic meeting of volunteer and permanent staff, chaired by Nick Hylton, which opted for a barquentine rig, or in other words a three-masted vessel with the square sails on the foremast.

One of Auckland's best-known yachtsman-designers, Don Brooke is the son of John Brooke, the architect of the *Spirit of Adventure*. Like Stephen Fisher, he could be said to represent the second generation of *Spirit* benefactors. Prior to taking on the *Spirit of New Zealand*, he had designed 15 steel sailing vessels between 21 and 28 metres and one 33.5-metre steel schooner. He was also the chairperson of the house committee of the Royal New Zealand Yacht Squadron.

Ted Ewbank's credentials were similarly impressive. A graduate of the Westlawn School of Yacht Design in the United States and also of the British Institute of Engineering Technology, he was a member of the Society of Naval Architects and Marine Engineers (United States), the Northeast Coast Institute of Engineers and Shipbuilders (United Kingdom) and the Institute of Nautical Surveyors (New Zealand). His previous design commissions included the general arrangement and major installations for the brigantine *Ji Fung* in Hong Kong, the general arrangement and steel hull structure of the replica of the *Bounty* (built in Whangarei and used in *The Bounty*, a large-budget Hollywood-financed film,

Opposite: *The hull of the* Spirit of New Zealand *gradually begins to take shape at Thackwray Yachts' yard in Te Atatu, West Auckland.*

starring Anthony Hopkins and Mel Gibson) and the hull design of the barge for the *Commodore of Auckland*.

The plans were completed in November 1982. By that time a name, *Spirit of New Zealand*, had been decided and the $2 million fund-raising campaign was well underway, including a nationwide promotional tour by the internationally acclaimed sailing celebrity, Peter Blake. Born in Auckland in 1948, already by the age of 34 Blake was New Zealand's most travelled blue-water yachtsman. He had sailed more than a quarter of a million nautical miles and competed in many ocean races, including three Whitbread round-the-world races. Today he has sailed over half a million miles—a tally that few sailors anywhere could equal. In 1990 he achieved a clean-sweep victory in his fifth Whitbread challenge, and in 1994 won the Jules Verne Trophy challenge, sailing non-stop around the world in just under 75 days. In 1982 Blake returned from England especially to take part in the fund-raising. The campaign was run from Stephen Fisher's office, with Tom Kenny as manager, and was enormously successful.

In March 1983 the Lottery Board of Control granted $150,000 from lottery funds for the *Spirit of New Zealand*. A house and beach section raffle organised by Neil Holdings and Challenge Properties raised a further $100,000 three months later. There were many individual and corporate donations, including a substantial endowment from Roy and Val Allen. The raffle of a new Rolls Royce (appropriately enough, a Silver Spirit) in December

Above: *The new hull of the* Spirit of New Zealand *being floated by tug to Marsden Wharf.*

Right: *The* Spirit of New Zealand *being fitted out at Marsden Wharf.*

1984 had great popular appeal, raising more than $650,000 towards the new ship. The Auckland man who won accidentally tossed the envelope containing his winning ticket into the rubbish, mistaking it for junk mail. Fortunately for him, it was retrieved by his wife.

The contract to build the *Spirit of New Zealand* went to Thackwray Yachts Ltd, an Auckland company which had hitherto specialised in the construction of large pleasure craft for overseas customers. Because of his eagerness for an example of the firm's workmanship to be seen in use in New Zealand waters, manager Phillip Thackwray took on the job for a smaller than usual profit margin. It was a fairly lengthy project for his shipwrights. The national president of the Voyagers Club, Kim Patterson, laid the keel at Thackwray's Te Atatu yard (15 kilometres northwest of Auckland city) on 18 November 1983, but it was not until 24 February 1986 that the ship was officially launched by solo yachtswoman Dame Naomi James. A further three months were needed to complete the complex rigging and fitting-out process at Marsden Wharf under the watchful eye of Nick Hylton, a full-time master with the trust.

Born in Gisborne, Naomi James became famous in 1978 when she shaved two days off Sir Francis Chichester's previous record of 117 days for a single-handed round-the-world yacht voyage. She was the first woman to round Cape Horn solo. A keen supporter of the *Spirit* programme, Dame Naomi had previously spoken at a fund-raising dinner in 1979.

Because of her dark hull, which contrasts sharply with the white formica bulkheads and handsome tawa and teak fittings, the new ship was soon nicknamed 'the Black Beauty'. With an overall length of 45.2 metres (more than 12 metres longer than *Spirit of Adventure*) and a beam of 9.1 metres (almost 3 metres wider than *Spirit of Adventure*), the *Spirit of New Zealand* is capable of carrying a maximum complement of 12 crew and 42 trainees. Below decks the eating quarters and officers' cabins are very spacious in comparison with the older ship. The twin dormitories for trainees make it possible for voyages to include equal numbers of boys and girls, whereas the more cramped conditions aboard the *Spirit of Adventure* in the early 1980s tended to favour single-sex voyages. Instead of the traditional great cabin or officers' mess at the stern, the *Spirit of New Zealand* has a large audio-visual theatre, which is ideal for lectures and briefing sessions. Able to consider in detail the time-proven merits and shortcomings of the *Spirit of Adventure*, the designers of the second ship created a splendidly seaworthy ocean-going vessel.

Her capabilities were put to the test very early on, for her sailing career began in atrocious weather. It was bad enough that the official launching by Dame Naomi and the tour of inspection by Prince Philip (who was again visiting New Zealand) took place on an unseasonably cold and wet summer's day. The two weekends of sea trials in July 1986 were conducted amidst particularly fierce and freezing southwesterly squalls. Nevertheless, towards the end of the first trial on 14 July, Nick Hylton, who had been a *Spirit of Adventure* master since 1979, managed to sail the new ship at an impressive 15 knots down the Waitemata Harbour. Hylton, an American married to a New Zealander, learned his trade crewing on big yachts, including the maxi-racer rivals *Ondine* and *Kialoa*, and ran a charter business in the Caribbean and the Pacific with his wife prior to working for the trust. Co-designer Ted Ewbank was on board that day to check how the rigging performed, but the most significant last-minute modification took place prior to embarking when a team of women Voyagers, volunteer and permanent crew worked hard and fast stowing lumps of pig iron in the hull to give the ship extra ballast.

A few further adjustments were necessary before the *Spirit of New Zealand* was ready to

The Spirit of New Zealand *was launched on 24 February 1986. Dame Naomi James, the Governor General, the Right Revd Sir Paul Reeves, Stephen Fisher, chairman of The Spirit of Adventure Trust, Virginia Fisher and Lady Reeves shelter beneath their brollies and wet weather gear.* (Cliff Hawkins)

Dame Naomi James launches the new ship. (Ron Bird)

Prince Philip, accompanied by Stephen Fisher, meets Ann Trenwith from the Operations Office (left) and trainees.

Early days: on her commissioning voyage, the Spirit of New Zealand ***reached speeds of over 10 knots as she sailed down Waitemata Harbour under Captain Nick Hylton's command.***

leave on her maiden voyage on 12 August 1986. In fact, a squad of engineers and electricians had to work all day on 11 August to fix a faulty alternator. A few of the engineers were still on board when the ship officially departed from Marsden Wharf at 4 p.m., but they were dropped off an hour or so later. Once again, the weather was at its worst on the day of departure, with non-stop rain all afternoon. The first issue of *The Spirit*, the trust's quarterly magazine, noted wryly in September 1986, 'When *Spirit of New Zealand* sailed on her maiden ten-day voyage, there wasn't a dry eye (or to be honest a dry anything) to be seen.' All the same, a large crowd gathered on Marsden Wharf to farewell her, including

SPIRIT OF
NEW ZEALAND

the band of the Royal New Zealand Air Force. In spite of the soggy start, the inaugural voyage, skippered again by Nick Hylton, was a great success. The ship was under full sail for the first time on the second day of the expedition.

The larger size of the *Spirit of New Zealand* made longer voyages possible. She embarked on her first circumnavigation of New Zealand in December 1986 and visited 14 ports during the next five months. In December 1987 she crossed the Tasman Sea from Bluff to Port Phillip Bay, Melbourne, and sailed to Hobart, where she officially represented New Zealand by taking part the following month in the Hobart to Sydney tall ships race, held to mark Australia's bicentenary. She finished second after the brigantine *Young Endeavour* (a bicentennial gift from Britain to Australia) in a field of 14 vessels from around the world. The ship also participated in the bicentennial celebrations in Sydney Harbour as an official New Zealand representative before resuming her normal voyaging duties in New Zealand in February 1987.

By all accounts, the Australian venture was a resounding success: the *Spirit of New Zealand* was greatly admired for her clean layout above and below decks, in particular the impressive 'amphitheatre' lecture-cum-dining area in the aft cabin. The four trainee crews proved to be excellent young ambassadors for New Zealand, and the mixed crews attracted much attention—especially from young South American sailors on the much larger naval training ships! John Duder, who was a crew member on the voyage, comments that he still doesn't know how, at the start of the race in Storm Bay off Hobart, Captain Nick Hylton managed to tack the ship in a flat calm—there was not even enough wind to blow the captain's pipe smoke away.

With two ships available, the trust could soon correct any lingering impression of an Auckland bias. The policy since late 1986 has been to vary the points of departure as much as possible so that at least one ship leaves on her ten-day voyage from a southern port. Of course, doubling the size of the fleet has also doubled the annual intake of trainees. More than doubled it, actually, because of the *Spirit of New Zealand*'s greater capacity. The intake rose immediately from 25 to 65 trainees every ten days. By July 1988 more than 10,000 trainees had passed through the programme. Currently the trust can accommodate more than 1400 youngsters per annum on the ten-day voyages.

Opposite top: *In Sydney Harbour, uniformed trainees on the* Spirit of New Zealand *gaze at some of the other tall ships that competed in the 610 nautical mile blue-water race from Hobart to Sydney as part of Australia's bicentennial celebrations in 1988. Visible (left to right) are* Nippon Maru *(Japan),* Gorch Fock *(Germany), the* Eagle *(USA),* Juan Sebastian de Elcano *(Spain) and* Dar Mlodziezy *(Poland).* (Cliff Hawkins)

Opposite bottom: *On 25 January 1988 the crews from the tall ships' race took part in a spectacular march through Sydney to the Opera House.* (Cliff Hawkins)

Opposite, clockwise from top left: *The wheel and main mast of the* Spirit of New Zealand. *Looking forward from the wheel along the main boom. The after compass (i.e., the one nearer the ship's stern). The belaying pins around the mizzen-mast. The port-side mizzen hoops.* Above: *The main mast (foreground), with the foremast behind.*

Chapter Four:
Awkward, Anxious and
Away from Home

The leading hand on the weekend voyage I joined in February 1994 was an assured and likeable 18-year-old of Chinese and Samoan descent named Maria Chan-Chui. Leading hands are young folk recruited from the Voyagers Club to serve as liaison points between the crew and the trainees. At the beginning of ten-day voyages, young people who have never sailed before often feel less embarrassed about seeking advice from someone more or less their own age rather than tackling an officer 20 or 30 years their senior. Even on adult 'weekenders', people new to sailing are generally reassured by the presence of someone aboard who has learned the fundamentals and can pass on helpful tips without appearing too intimidatingly experienced. Maria's nautical know-how was very fresh in her mind, because she had returned just a couple of weeks earlier from her first voyage on the *Spirit of Adventure* as a raw trainee.

I asked her what she had enjoyed so much about that first voyage to make her want to sail again so soon afterwards. 'Oh, I made so many friends,' she immediately replied. When I asked her to estimate approximately how many, she smiled and said, 'The whole ship! I got to know all the trainees—and the officers too.'

This, I later found, is a common response from ex-trainees. Invited to comment on the chief pleasures of sailing on the *Spirits*, they almost always begin by talking about the friendships they forged. That and the joy of watching dolphins.

About 34 species of cetaceans inhabit New Zealand waters. Although many different

No voyage is complete without them: dolphins frolic off Cape Palliser (SOA voyage 419). (Greg Walker)

On day one of their voyage, with the ship still moored at Marsden Wharf, trainees have a first go at climbing aloft.

varieties have been spotted by trainees from time to time, particularly on voyages along the Pacific coastline, it tends to be the most common dolphin (*Delphinus delphis*) which provokes the most squeals of delight from the young people on board the *Spirit* ships. Why is this marine mammal more popular with them than any other sea creature? I think the answer is that the *Delphinus delphis* always appears in a big fun-loving group. Whereas fish and seabirds seem somewhat dour as they go about their business (which consists mainly of eating one another), the dolphins appear to devote themselves entirely to a life of ceaseless frolicking. They represent a vision of freedom—a neverending playtime, one might say—to the chore-bound trainees.

When 17-year-old Robert Searle from Lytton High boarded the *Spirit of Adventure* in January 1993, he discovered that the young people's home addresses ranged from Whanga-paraoa in the north to Te Anau in the south, but he was the only one from the Gisborne area. In a report he later wrote for the Gisborne newspaper the *Eastland Sun*, he admitted to feeling a little awkward and bashful at first, but he went on to say, 'You meet heaps of people and end up being really good mates. If you start off shy, you don't end up shy.'

Newspapers up and down the country frequently ask local trainees to write about their experience aboard the ships. Robert's report is typical. 'I met some really awesome people of my own age from north of Auckland right down to Southland, and from a wide range of backgrounds,' Melanie Bell, a 17-year-old from Gisborne Girls High School who sailed on the *Spirit of New Zealand*, told the *Gisborne Herald* in February 1994.

'Over a period of ten days I made friends I will never forget!' Tammi Shapcott from Rangiora High School (27 kilometres north of Christchurch) enthused in the Christchurch newspaper *Outlook North Canterbury* in January 1993. 'By day eight we were all really close, and it was hard to imagine that a week ago none of us knew each other. Now it felt like we had all known each other for years,' Raewyn Scott of Stanmore Bay (a residential area and seaside summer resort on the Whangaparaoa Peninsula, 41 kilometres northeast of Auckland) informed the *Hibiscus Coaster* in September 1992. Dozens of similar testimonies from recent years could be added to this small selection.

During ten days of facing continual challenges together, the trainees invariably get to know everybody on board pretty well. There's nowhere on a sailing ship that you can hide yourself for long. Even people who are normally bashful and retiring are forced to socialise. You can't haul on ropes together for hours or stand in the same small galley washing and drying mountains of dishes together without saying a word. It's just not human nature. Everybody involved in the *Spirit* programme, from the trainees up to the trustees, will tell you that tolerance, co-operation, social confidence and amiability are among the most important lessons to be learned aboard the two ships.

The learning process is gradual, however. The trainees are almost always very wary of one another to begin with. The first few hours aboard either of the ships can be the loneliest of their young lives. Not only are they separated from their families and friends, but there are no familiar faces at all. The watch bill (the list of trainees) on each ten-day voyage is carefully compiled by the operations office so that every trainee comes from a different part of the country. A typical mix would include young people from provincial centres like Whangarei, Tauranga, Napier, Palmerston North, Nelson and Invercargill and small towns like Kaitaia (New Zealand's northernmost borough), Te Awamutu, Putaruru, Geraldine, Mosgiel and Winton, as well as the main cities.

Experience has shown that acquaintances from the same area, if allowed on the same voyage, tend to form a clique which closes off from the rest of the group. As it is, all the trainees are on the same footing, regardless of where they come from. Everybody has to reach out and make new friends.

Not many are bold enough to reach out straightaway. On the first morning, as they wait on the deck for further instructions, the trainees eye one another nervously with brief side-ways glances but avoid making contact. Most of them have their heads down and their arms folded in a defensive posture. Although space on the deck is limited, they try to keep as much distance from one another as possible. Some chew their nails. Others pick at imaginary lint on their clothing. Only a few feel confident enough to speak to their neighbours, even though there's no shortage of questions they could ask one another. What's

Dressed in the distinctive, bright yellow 'banana skins', these trainees on SOA voyage 438 have their first taste of going out on the yard in October 1992. (Tina Aarsen)

your name? Which school are you from? Whereabouts is that? Are you in the fifth form or the sixth or the seventh? How old are you exactly? Have you ever sailed before? What do you think of the ship? Are you as scared as I am? How many chocolate bars do you have stashed away in your pack? In time the flood of queries will come. No trainee yet has managed to maintain an unbroken ten-day silence. But the first morning is almost always spookily quiet. Even if it's an overcast day, sunglasses tend to stay firmly in place to prevent uneasy eye contact with the shipload of strangers.

As they arrive at the wharf, the trainees are welcomed by one of the watch officers and a leading hand. Generally what happens in this first encounter is that the officer and leading hand beam encouragingly, going out of their way to show that they won't bite, and the trainee responds, if he or she responds at all, with a glum tight-lipped twitching of the mouth. A busy wharf is a frightening place when you've just come from Okaihau College in the far north (in the Bay of Islands county) or Tokomairiro High School (in South Otago) and you've never been alone in a big city before.

There are several pieces of administrative business to be fulfilled. Names and dates of birth must be checked. Wet-weather gear and folders of literature pertaining to the voyage must be issued. Medical certificates must be collected and checked, if these have not already been posted through to the operations office. The trainees' faces, already apprehensive, generally become more anxious still at the mention of wet-weather gear. When they have pictured the voyage to themselves in the weeks prior to embarkation, they have usually imagined themselves basking in glorious sunshine. The idea that they might spend the next ten days in howling winds and pelting rain is new to most of them—and an absolutely appalling thought. More often than not, they don't say anything, beyond a morose and not particularly sincere 'Thanks', when they receive the bright yellow jackets and leggings (commonly known as 'banana skins'), but their hearts really become heavy. Those with inquisitive fingers often find in the pockets of the jackets soggy handkerchiefs left behind by waterlogged trainees on a previous voyage. These heirlooms are more than a little offputting too.

Some of the younger trainees are not only new to sailing, they have never before set foot on a boat of any kind. They can be spotted easily by the gingerly way they cross the gangway for the first time, clinging tightly to their wet-weather gear, bags and folders. Experienced sailors seldom bother to think twice about the sturdiness of gangways. They spring across them with a couple of casual bounds. Novices, however, tend to look at how high and narrow these passages are and worry about them breaking under their feet. The first few steps, made in expectation of imminent disaster, are often very tentative.

All the trainees are given berth numbers and assigned to one watch or another as they arrive. Most of them need to be reminded again later which watch they are part of, but the berth numbers are crucial when they first board the ships because they need to know right away where to store their luggage. By and large, the trainees are dismayed when they first clap eyes on their bunks and lockers. Are they really supposed, they wonder, to live in these cramped conditions for the best part of a fortnight? On the *Spirit of Adventure* the two dormitories, positioned on either side of the hull, with a steel wall separating the boys from the girls, can each accommodate 13 people. On the *Spirit of New Zealand* each of the twin dormitories can sleep 21 people. The trainees don't actually spend much of their time in these quarters. The bunks are just somewhere to collapse exhausted at the end of a long day. They are perfectly adequate for this purpose. When the trainees first spy them, however, they imagine that the next ten days will be like sharing a tiny bedroom with a dozen or more strangers, some of whom might turn out to have weird and disgusting habits.

That's why almost all of them are in a very sober frame of mind by the time they congregate on the aft deck to await whatever calamity is next going to befall them. The great majority have trouble at first adjusting to the confined space. Country kids who have come from big farms, where they are accustomed to striding powerfully across the paddocks, find it difficult to scale down their movements so that they don't get in the way of their shipmates. Not that they are necessarily clumsier than city-bred teenagers, who might well be less used to physical exercise and consequently much less fit.

Because the trainees travel to the ships from all over New Zealand, it's impossible to ensure that they all arrive at the wharf at the same time. Flights and coach trips are sometimes delayed unavoidably by weather conditions. Ten-day voyages usually begin on a Tuesday, with provisioning and minor maintenance and repairs carried out the previous day. Trainees who have to undergo long journeys before they join the ships usually arrive on Monday and are billeted overnight. Most of the billets have a fairly close connection to the *Spirit* programme, either through the operations office or the board or the Supporters Club or the Voyagers. These people recognise the importance of observing the scheduled

Opposite: *The* Spirit of New Zealand, *with master Nick Hylton at the helm, departs from Marsden Wharf, Auckland, at the beginning of a voyage.*

Trainees are encouraged to keep the Spirit *ships spick-and-span at all times. This includes hosing down the decks, scrubbing the galley, polishing all the brass, and even sweeping along the outside of the ship. It is only because the* Spirit of Adventure *is at anchor that the intrepid sweeper shown here is not wearing a harness.* (Top right and opposite, top left and right: Alfred Memelink)

boarding times as closely as possible. It's not uncommon, though, for out-of-towners to be welcomed at airports or bus stations by their relatives. If it's many years since you last saw young Tom or Janet, or (to make matters even more acute) if this is the first time you have ever met them, and you want to prove just what a splendid aunt or uncle you are, the natural thing is to go on a little sightseeing tour. Some of these end up not being so little after all. The really extended ones have been known to delay the ships' departures for hours.

Some trainees have sat up all night on trains. Others have been up at dawn to catch planes. Travelling alone by bus and plane, with all the accompanying anxieties about luggage, is a frightening adventure in itself for young people who have always previously relied on their parents to handle the technicalities. Staying overnight in a strange house can be unnerving too, especially if you're naturally rather shy. By the time they assemble on the aft deck, some trainees are already feeling a bit worn out from all the worries and culture shock of the last day and night. Others are impatient for all the waiting around to be over and done with and the voyage to begin in earnest.

Although the intention is always to depart from the wharf as soon as possible, many things must be checked before a sailing ship is ready for sea. Is the navigational equipment working properly? Are the radar, radios and other electronics in good repair? Are there any problems with the sails? Has all the food for the voyage been brought on board and stored away correctly? Is everybody present and accounted for? The checking process can seem neverending to the young trainees, especially those who arrived at the wharf bright and early.

Even as the crew conduct the final checks on the electronics, the trainees might feel as if they have been unplugged. For the next ten days there will be no video games, no television and no CD players. As Bill McCook puts it, 'We put young people back in a time warp of three miles an hour. You can't solve the problems on a sailing ship with a computer or a calculator.'

The trainees have plenty of time to review their decision to sign on board. All the trainees are there by choice. There are about 400 secondary schools in New Zealand and nearly all of them support the *Spirit* programme. About 95 per cent of the berths on the ships are allocated to secondary schools. Any teacher can nominate suitable candidates, but in most cases the students are also required to make some kind of written application. The selection process varies from school to school. In some of the country's larger secondary institutions, competition for the available berths is strong enough among students to warrant a formal procedure whereby candidates are interviewed by a panel of selectors. It should be stressed, however, that The Spirit of Adventure Trust has always advised teachers that young people lacking a little in self-confidence might benefit more from the voyages than those who have already proven themselves high achievers.

Some school principals have opted for less solemn methods when making the final decisions. The operations office allocated one berth on the *Spirit of New Zealand*'s maiden voyage in August 1986 to Okato College (on the northwestern foot of Mt Taranaki). Two lads were equally keen to sail and both seemed equally worthy. The school principal, David Carroll, decided who it was going to be by tossing a coin—as fair-minded an approach as any other and far quicker than most.

At one time, voyages made during the school holidays were filled with nominees from the Supporters Club. Nowadays the Supporters' selections are integrated throughout the year with school-based trainees. A few of the trainees come into the category 'youth at risk' and have been referred to the trust by the Justice Department. Increasingly, too, young people with minor physical handicaps have been encouraged to participate in ordinary voyages, although special expeditions are still arranged on a regular basis for those with more severe disabilities, such as blindness, paraplegia, profound deafness or insulin-reliant diabetes, where extra surveillance and medical attention are required. With few exceptions, there is a place for all young people 15 years and older who wish or need to take the *Spirit* challenge.

The general aim is to bring as many different types as possible together on each voyage. One of the most striking statements I have seen about the variety of trainees comes from Charlotte Gardner, who in April 1993 wrote an article for the *Cambridge Independent* about a voyage from Lyttelton to Wellington on the *Spirit of New Zealand* that she participated in as a sixth-former. 'There was a broad spectrum of personalities on the ship,' she wrote. 'They ranged from students who attended private schools through to the other end

The **Spirit of New Zealand,** *Great Barrier Island.*

of the scale, a boy who was the possessor of six tattoos and commented as we sailed past Wellington's Mt Crawford Prison about the various members of his family who have, over the years, been imprisoned there.' (On the Miramar Peninsula, about 10 kilometres from Wellington City, Mt Crawford is 163 metres high, with the prison near the summit.)

The full cost of a ten-day voyage is around $1125 per person, but the trust currently charges each trainee only $697 and subsidises the rest. For many young people, though, $697 (all inclusive) is still a lot of money to be raised. The majority of the trainees rely, at least partly, on sponsorship either from their schools' discretionary funds or from local service clubs. The Fiordland Rotary Club in the far south, for example, sponsors at least one trainee every year from Fiordland College. The Dargaville Lions Club sponsors someone annually from Dargaville High School. Every year the Jaycees Club of Whakatane organises a 'Spelrite' competition which features pages of advertising with deliberate mistakes in them. The person who identifies the most errors is the winner and the money raised from the advertising revenue goes towards sending four local youngsters on *Spirit* voyages.

In some parts of the country, several organisations will unite in their efforts to sponsor a trainee. In 1993, for instance, Melanie Bell from Gisborne Girls High School was jointly sponsored by her school, her local dog trial club, several local sports clubs, the Tiniroto Community Association and the local branch of the Stockyards Association. It's not unusual for dairies, grocery shops, service stations and other small businesses to assist by offering paid part-time work to high school students. Some service clubs organise weekend adult voyages aboard the *Spirit* ships with the stipulation that part of the proceeds will go

61

towards sponsoring young people from their area on ten-day voyages. In May 1993, for instance, the Rotary Club of Picton booked the *Spirit of Adventure* for a weekend voyage around the Marlborough Sounds and were thereby able to pay the fees of two local youngsters.

Some organisations specialise in helping young people who otherwise would be unable to pay. The New Zealand Royal Ex-Navalmen's Association sponsors one such trainee a year. The John Wallace McKenzie Trust, set up in 1989 by the law firm Russell McVeagh McKenzie Bartleet & Co in memory of their late senior partner (a founding member of The Spirit of Adventure Trust), has fully or partially funded more than 150 young people from financially disadvantaged families.

It would take a long time to list all of the philanthropic organisations in New Zealand which have given financial support over the last 21 years to trainees, because not only do they include the various branches of the Lions, Rotarians, Jaycees and Returned Servicemen's Association but also harbour boards, local businesses, regional divisions of the Motor Vehicle Dealers Institute, dog trial clubs, sports groups and volunteer fire brigades. There's a tremendous amount of community goodwill towards the *Spirit* programme throughout the country. Of course, the sponsorship or work-related funding also has a psychological effect on the trainees. They arrive at the wharf with the weight of social responsibility on their shoulders because, beyond themselves, they are representing not just their schools but their whole districts. As they listen to the captain's introductory speech on the first morning, many of the trainees are feeling homesick and wishing they had never put their names forward for this nautical ordeal. But the more mature ones also feel that they can't let themselves or the people back home down—all those who parted with hard-earned dollars to pay for their berths—by fleeing overboard at the earliest opportunity.

Actually, there's only one known instance of someone fleeing overboard and he wasn't a trainee but a young first-time cook seconded from the Trentham army camp (31 kilometres northeast of Wellington) for a voyage on the *Spirit of Adventure* from Wellington to Lyttelton in March 1991. Lying awake in the dark in his cabin on the first night, when the ship was moored off Kau Bay at the northern end of the Wellington Harbour, the unfortunate fellow began to suffer from serious claustrophobia. Clad only in shorts and a T-shirt, he scrambled up on deck in panic, leapt over the side and swam the 100 metres or so to shore. He walked the coastal roads for some time, before he was picked up by the police. He did not return to the ship.

The only other possible absconder was Scuppers, the ship's cat, a cute short-haired tabby who survived only five voyages. Her first was voyage 30 in May 1975. She was posted as missing in the ship's log, presumably lost overboard, on 24 July 1975, on the third day of voyage 35.

During the first few hours aboard, the trainees not infrequently feel like absconding. Two seventh-formers at Dunedin's Bayfield High, Ellen Mary Pullar and Steven Parker, who had recently completed voyages on the *Spirit of New Zealand*, were interviewed in April 1993 for the school's newspaper. 'On the first day of the trip,' said the *Bayleaf*, both Steven and Ellen admitted to being 'scared and freaked out, and wanting to go home'.

For many, these feelings intensify during the next few days, when they are smitten with seasickness (not to mention homesickness) and their hands and arm muscles have not yet become used to pulling on ropes. About day four, for the vast majority, the mood begins to change. By day eight they are really enjoying themselves, and on the final day some almost need to be prised from the spars.

Chapter Five:
Learning the Ropes

Changes in the personnel, the weather and the destinations ensure that no two voyages aboard the *Spirit of Adventure* or the *Spirit of New Zealand* are ever the same. The trust's manual of standing orders and operational procedures states that 'all those on board are considered to be members of the crew'. The ships carry no dead weight. Judged from this perspective, the crew is ever-changing, with a fresh complement of sailors every time either ship departs. The permanent officers vary too, since even the most fervently maritime of the trust's employees occasionally feel the need for some shore leave between voyages. And there's a large pool of volunteers who are willing to devote their services as officers free of charge when their time is available. As the people change, so of course do the social dynamics, making each voyage a unique and unrepeatable experience.

Although careful attention is always paid to weather forecasts, it's impossible to be certain in advance exactly what the weather will be like ten days hence. Some trainees have been blessed with glorious sunshine throughout their voyage. Others have been obliged to contend with almost non-stop wind and rain. It's not uncommon for trainees on the same voyage to spend one day utterly becalmed and another coping with 50-knot gales. Sailing ships are more reliant on weather conditions than any other form of transport. Even if two voyages take place in the same general area, such as the inner Hauraki Gulf, the wind is unlikely to be identical on both occasions. And if the wind is different, so is the whole sailing experience.

Sailing in rough weather can be exciting. Probably the worst weather for a sailing ship are days that are both wet and windless. The trainees are forced inside to listen to lectures.

*Aloft on SONZ voyage 134
in Cook Strait, May 1992.*
(Belinda McPherson)

Left: *In spite of a blustery day in Cook Strait, the* Spirit of Adventure *performs beautifully.* (Alfred Memelink)

Right: *A native of Omaha, Nebraska, Nick Hylton is one of the trust's longest serving masters, first signing on in December 1978. He did much to establish the style and tone of the* Spirit *voyages.*

One of the things that young trainees are keenest to know on their first day aboard is where on earth they are going. During his years as master, Nick Hylton used to reply to that query by saying, 'Wherever the wind takes us.' He was only partly teasing. He was well aware of the range of possibilities, but, to use the Hauraki Gulf as an example again, it would depend on the kind of wind power available whether Hylton would be able to take the ship as far as Great Barrier Island (about 90 kilometres north of Marsden Wharf) or sail only about a quarter of that distance, keeping mainly within sight of Waiheke Island. He wasn't prepared to cheat by just motoring out to Great Barrier Island regardless of the weather conditions. If you don't use the teamwork to at least try to sail, it defeats the whole purpose of a sail training programme.

'Every opportunity should be taken, within reasonable safety limits, to provide interesting and exhilarating sailing,' says the 1977 *Instructor's Handbook*. 'Motor sailing is no substitute; there is little sailing knowledge to be gained and sail changes are severely restricted under these conditions—not to mention the fact that diesel costs more than wind!' After pointing out that the ship should try to manoeuvre under sail even when berthing, slipping, anchoring and weighing, the manual adds another stern reminder: 'The *Spirit of Adventure*'s main propulsion comes from above the deck not below it!'

A voyage around the Hauraki Gulf is a very different experience from a coastal journey from Lyttelton to Dunedin or from Dunedin to Bluff. A voyage departing from Queen's

Wharf in Wellington Harbour (where 30-knot northwesterlies are not uncommon), crossing Cook Strait, exploring the Marlborough Sounds and then returning to Wellington will be very different in character from one which departs from Gisborne, sails round the Coromandel Peninsula and eventually arrives at Marsden Wharf. Because of the necessity of reaching a particular destination on a particular date, some voyages begin with two days of non-stop sailing. Hampered by bad weather, others do not leave port at all on the first day. The journey from Gisborne to Whitianga on the Coromandel Peninsula has generally been accomplished as a two-day straight sail. Cook Strait, on the other hand, is often too rough for trainees to tackle on their first day, so they anchor instead at Petone and spend a couple of days learning to sail in Wellington Harbour.

In short, there's no such thing as a typical voyage. Each one is singular and exceptional. Certain features are common to them all, however. The trust's standing orders make clear that the chief responsibility of the captain is the 'safety and appearance of the ship and those on board from the ship's departure until her return alongside'. Thus, no matter where the voyage is bound, prior to departure the master always addresses everyone on board on the subject of safety procedures. Usually this introductory lecture, which covers such topics as life rafts, life jackets, fire extinguishers and how crucial the wearing of harnesses is in rough weather, on the bowsprit or when going aloft, will be kept fairly brief so that trainees are not overburdened with detail. There are ground rules to be established. Trainees aren't to smoke, drink, chew gum or swear. They don't sit on the rails, the life rafts, the cabin roof

Safety is a primary concern on any voyage. One of the mates, Barbara White, shows trainees the correct way to put on their life jackets.

or the life jackets. They don't go aloft without permission or a safety harness. They don't throw anything overboard or fiddle with the knobs in the wheelhouse.

Experienced officers, like senior master Paul Leppington, who first sailed on the *Spirit of Adventure* as a first mate in April 1975, develop a sixth sense for how much information trainees can absorb at a single stretch. Key points are carefully reinforced as the voyage advances. I've frequently heard former trainees speak about Paul Leppington with obvious affection as well as respect. 'He somehow knew how to get on our wavelength,' they say.

The first contact between officers and trainees is important for setting the right tone. The ideal officer is a mixture of discipline and approachability. Discipline is unavoidable on a sailing ship. Hoisting a sail is only possible with teamwork, with everyone knowing what to do and doing it. If people can't be bothered, the ship won't move. But it's also essential that trainees should feel free to ask questions whenever they are uncertain. There ought to

Left: *Preparing to hoist the staysails on the* Spirit of New Zealand. (Donna MacIntosh)

Right: *National fundraiser Vaughan Robertson shows leader manager participant Helene McKenzie the correct method of coiling lines on SONZ voyage 118DP.*

Opposite: *A confident team tends the sails on the starboard side of the* Spirit of Adventure. (Alfred Memelink)

be an atmosphere of mutual respect rather than coercion and resentment. So the officer wants to treat trainees as individuals, getting to know their names quickly. It should be implied that high standards are expected and slacking won't be tolerated. The whole idea is for people to rise to meet challenges. Anybody can perform an easy chore in fine weather after a good night's sleep. But it can't be Bligh-like, as if people will be keelhauled or given the cat-o'-nine-tails if they step out of line.

An address Prince Philip gave to the Sail Training Association has become a classic definition of what it takes to be a good officer: 'With the exception of a military situation, sail training is the most demanding of tasks associated with the sea—it is also the most rewarding. It requires of its officers the continual practice of a high standard of seamanship, unlimited resources of patience, understanding and tolerance, the utmost reliability and integrity, a sense of humour—but, above all, the mental resolve and physical strength capable of pure, unadulterated bloody hard work!'

The division of the trainees into three or four watches is the other essential business to be sorted out prior to departure. On the *Spirit of Adventure* each watch consists of eight trainees (supervised by an adult watch officer) and on the *Spirit of New Zealand* each is ten strong (plus the watch officer). They take turns in manning the various stations on the ship—foredeck, midships, mainsail and specials (i.e., cooking, laying the table, washing cooking utensils, peeling potatoes, and navigation). At some point during the voyage, every trainee has a turn at being watch leader, which might mean being in charge of putting up, taking down or adjusting a sail or just supervising the peeling of potatoes, depending on circumstances.

Writing for her local newspaper, the *Hibiscus Coaster*, in September 1992, 18-year-old Serean Adams from Red Beach said of a recent voyage around the Hauraki Gulf in the *Spirit of Adventure*, 'Mains tends to stick out in my mind as being the busiest station, where crew members have to tend the sheets of the main and mainstay sails while at the same time bracing the yards and taking care of the running backstays.' She might be right, but none of the stations qualifies as a 'cushy number' and trainees may find some more arduous, or at least more disagreeable, than others, especially if the duties include cleaning the toilets (known as 'the heads', perhaps rather confusingly, since this is not the part of the anatomy usually associated with them).

Just getting the hang of the nautical terminology, which Serean employs so adeptly in her report, is a major challenge for most trainees during the first few days. In normal land-based life a sheet is a large rectangular piece of fabric. Logically, therefore, you would think that when sailors refer to 'sheets' they must be talking about the sails. But in maritime parlance the term 'sheet' does not mean the sail itself but the rope attached to the outer corner of the sail to secure it or control its angle to the wind. You must not lapse into the erroneous belief that all ropes are sheets, however. Ropes used for hoisting and lowering things, instead of just changing their direction, aren't called sheets but halyards (literally, haul-yards). Small pieces of rope used for odd jobs aren't called sheets or halyards but ties or gaskets.

According to an estimate made a few years ago by one trainee, Michael Tappenden of Otorohanga, the *Spirit of New Zealand* contains 240 ropes (whatever you want to call them) and over half a hectare of sail. Each rope has a different function and a different name, but they all look pretty much the same to an untutored eye.

One of the first lessons trainees learn is the importance of keeping sheets and halyards in a tidy condition at all times, coiled in even-sized loops round the belaying pins (metal

Hoisting the headsail on the
Spirit of New Zealand.

cleats) and tightly secured. These ropes are the ship's controls. If they become entangled, it's impossible to change the direction of the sails (and, consequently, the ship) at short notice to take advantage of favourable winds. Loose ends are also dangerous. In wet weather it's hard enough to walk around or avoid hazards on an uncluttered deck, let alone one that's full of snags, snares and debris to trip over.

But since good sailing depends on making continual adjustments to the sails, as soon as a length of rope is snugly coiled and fastened, more often than not it needs to be let out again. Beginners can find this process very frustrating. Some of their most beautifully executed loops and coils are so short lived, alas, that they pass entirely unnoticed and unpraised by the officers. Eventually the process of tying up loose ends becomes automatic.

A delightful account of a novice's confusion aboard the *Spirit of Adventure* was written for the *Wairarapa News* in January 1993 by Janet Drummond, an adult journalist who participated on a day sail around Wellington Harbour. 'A teenage girl would call out, "Take the rope" and we would grab it as though having a tug-of-war. Then came the call "Heave!" and we would heave like mad, almost falling over each other. After the third heaving, I realised the sail was actually turning round and we were going in a different direction. Probably one of the crew had explained all this, but with the wind making a terrific noise in the sails and the ropes going ping ping ping against the masts it was almost impossible to hear anything.'

There's a competitive element, of course, to dividing the ship into watches. The four teams strive for the next ten days to outperform one another. But the watch system isn't just a matter of boosting productivity through rivalry. It also makes the ship less intimidating for the individual trainee. Everyone has a group that he or she belongs to and shares experiences with. When the trainees are making friends, generally they begin with the others in their watch and then radiate out from that central core to encompass the rest of the ship's personnel.

However, even within the same watch it usually takes two or three days for friendships to crystallise. The first day on board can seem very long and lonely, especially for the group required to serve as the night watch. Watch duties continue round the clock on the *Spirit* ships. The trainees are expected to take their turns in the wheelhouse in the wee hours before dawn. The concept of a broken night's sleep is new to most of the young people and few adapt to it quickly and graciously. On the first night trainees may make the mistake of clambering off to bed as soon as they have woken those who are to take over from them, with the risk that the replacements utter a loud oath at being roused and then go back to sleep again, leaving the wheelhouse unattended by trainees for the next hour so. The correct method is to wait until your reliever has safely arrived on the deck before you collapse. The more tired you are, the more discipline this takes. They check the anchor bearings at half-hourly intervals and record them in the log, as well as wind direction, wind speed, barometer readings, air temperatures. They report to the duty officer any boats coming alongside.

Although they are often loath to admit it, many of the trainees have never been awake at 4 a.m. or 5 a.m. or dawn prior to their commitment as part of the night watch. There's no such thing as a completely silent ship. The creaks and groans can be spooky when you're standing alone on a darkened deck, even if you know the ship is anchored in a placid harbour and there's no way for intruders to come aboard without telltale splashes. The watches are usually conducted in pairs. But since voices carry so easily at night conversations need to be whispered and kept to a minimum. Solitude is a difficult art to master if you're naturally garrulous and gregarious.

Even in broad daylight the *Spirit* ships are rather intimidating. There are so many ropes and they all have individual names—topsail buntline, mainstay handy billy, raffee sheet, main staysail halyard, upper fisherman throat, lower fisherman sheet. The names of the ropes are engraved on the metal cleats to which they are attached, but what on earth do they mean? It's bad enough for someone terrified of knots to be asked to tie a bowline in anything, let alone the starboard flying jib sheet.

Gradually, however, the nomenclature begins to make sense. From eavesdropping on

Opposite: *The view from aloft on the* Spirit of New Zealand *at dawn.*

the captain's conferences with the first and second mates about whether it's worth adding the raffee or the upper fisherman, you start to appreciate the functions of the different sails. Each sail has several ropes attached to it to help pull it into the desired direction depending on wind conditions.

At first, when you don't have a clue what you're doing, hauling on ropes all day long is a bore. It's hard not to entertain treacherous thoughts that all the rapturous effusions about the romance of sails are just bunkum, the steam engine was a marvellous invention and the aeroplane an even better one. Then slowly your eyes become accustomed to following the line that you're working with, instead of just surrendering at the sight of so much complicated rigging above your head. You can see which way a particular sail ought to be set in order to catch the wind. When you begin making spontaneous suggestions to the first mate about the trimming of the flying jib, you know that you're finally getting the hang of sailing.

Which is the worst time slot on deck? Midnight to 0200 (the nautical term for 2 a.m.) is pretty bad, because you probably won't get much sleep beforehand. But 0200–0400 is probably worse, because whatever sleep you manage to get will be broken into fits and snatches. Worst of all may be 0400–0600, because just as you're about to creep wearily back to your bunk for a few hours' shuteye, you realise that it's time for PT, the dawn swim, breakfast and another day. In that slot, however, you do at least have the minor revenge of waking up everyone else.

Celestina Phillips was a 17-year-old correspondence school student living at the Patea hydro dam (in Taranaki) when she took part in a *Spirit of Adventure* voyage from Whangarei to Auckland in September 1992. She recorded some comments about her first night watch for the *Wanganui Chronicle*. 'We were rostered in pairs for two hours at a time,' she explained, 'to keep an eye out at night. We had to make sure the anchor didn't scrape the bottom, or no one came on board. It was exciting. On the first shift watch my partner and I heard strange noises. It sounded like someone in the water with breathing apparatus on. We woke our watch officer who scanned the area and reassured us it was probably only dolphins or a whale.'

Tired as they are after a long and stressful day hauling on ropes, the trainees sometimes take a while to fall asleep on the first night, even if they are free from wheelhouse duties and fears about invading divers. For most of them, the fold down canvas hammocks compare unfavourably with the comforts of home. It's not easy to sit up, curl up or roll over in the rather constricted bunks and getting in and out of bed is a trapeze-like act, especially for the person on the top level. Although a steel bulkhead separates the boys' and girls' dormitories, voices can nevertheless carry at night from one side of the ship to the other. Young Robert Searle from Gisborne told the *Eastland Sun* in January 1993, 'We could hear the girls talking about us, which was quite funny.'

It's strictly forbidden for any two people on board to share the same bunk. Anybody caught trying is sent home without completing the voyage. Parents can relax, however. Only a pair of exceptionally small and brazen contortionists could manage to engage in any untoward activities within these confined and very public hammocks.

Joanna Graham wrote an article for *NZ Yachting and Power Boating* in 1977. It still holds true. 'The first problem we all found was lack of space. This became obvious on our first night when we all got ready for bed and in the morning (0600 hours) when we got up. People were crawling out of sleeping bags, queuing up for the best pump toilet, having washes; arms poking everywhere trying to get into clothes.' One bunk in the forward mess-

Warm-up exercises and a plunge into the ocean at dawn are part of every voyage. Refreshing it may be, but it's good to get back on board!

deck, she noted, was nicknamed 'the coffin'. She raised eyebrows by recording 'We made a new record—17 girls streaked once around the ship.' (This was a segregated voyage.)

Come dawn, however, and the prospect of plunging into the freezing brine, the bunks suddenly don't seem so bad. Summer, autumn, winter and spring, the trainees and at least one officer are obliged to begin the day in their swimsuits with a series of brisk warm-up exercises on the deck (lasting about 10 to 15 minutes) followed by a swim off the ship. On winter mornings, nobody needs to be told to swim briskly. It's a mad scramble to be the first back on board with a towel draped around your quivering goosebumps. The sea can seem so cold that it takes your breath away. It's the air temperature rather than the sea temperature which is the real problem, however, and accordingly officers must be vigilant.

There's nothing like the dawn swim for reminding trainees that they are not on a luxury cruise. 'A giant black bath,' is how it was described by Natasha Jones who participated in a mid-winter voyage around the Hauraki Gulf on the *Spirit of Adventure* in June 1992. 'A nightmare for sleeper-inners' was another description. There's a rule that at least one of the officers must be prepared to take the plunge too. 'Never ask a trainee to do what you would not do yourself,' says the *Instructor's Handbook*. If the seas are too rough or too infested with jellyfish, if the ship is moving, or if all the permanent crew chicken out, the swim is called off.

As well as cleaning and refreshing trainees, the morning dip often inspires them to eat heartier than usual breakfasts, devouring large platefuls of sausages, scrambled eggs, cereal and toast. Having such a full stomach at the beginning of the day is not always a wise idea. An outsize breakfast is also a delaying tactic, of course, prolonging the start to another long day of sailing, working aloft, hauling, winching and knot-tying. The morning meal is invariably followed, however, by a thorough clean-up of the ship and the ceremony known as colours—the hoisting of the New Zealand flag and the traditional ringing of eight bells at 0800. Then each watch reports for duty at its designated sail station for the next 24 hours.

Chapter Six:
In Sickness and in Health

Every morning, just before colours, all hands assemble on the aft deck for a briefing by the master or mate on the likely weather conditions, the range of options and the course planned for the day ahead. The accent is on the first syllable: presail briefings are kept brief. One could begin by explaining how differences in barometric pressure cause winds and by comparing the types of cloud and the reasons for the differences. Or the principles of aerodynamics. Why it is that some sails are pushers while others are suckers. Or luff tension, sag and stretch. But boredom and inattention set in quickly after about 30 minutes. The general philosophy on the *Spirits* is that people learn best by doing. The most fruitful discussions follow practical experience rather than precede it. Thus, instead of lecturing the trainees at length every morning on the theory of sailing, it's preferable to have them hoist some canvas as soon as possible and get the ship moving. Questions (such as 'Where did you say this rope is supposed to go?') will arise naturally.

On the second day, most of the trainees have forgotten everything they were told on the first. It was all too new and frightening and alien to be absorbed in one go. The officers are prepared for this kind of amnesia, because it happens on every voyage. 'Explain the task several times as necessary for the trainee to understand,' says the *Instructor's Handbook*. 'If the task is done wrongly, it is usually due to inadequate explanation. Always before or after a task, explain why (later the trainee should be asked to tell the officer why).' Often it's not until the fourth or fifth day that the trainees really begin to understand what they're doing. As well as the difficulty of having to cope with so much novelty all at once, there is

Left: *The classic death row —trainees on SOA voyage 389 under the weather, both figuratively and literally, in Cook Strait.* (Greg Walker)

Next page: *Trainees on SONZ voyage 173 heave to off Great Barrier Island.*

something else during the first few days which impairs the trainees' rate of learning. Many of them aren't feeling at all well.

Did Abel Tasman, James Cook and the legendary Maori navigator Kupe ever succumb to seasickness? It's not a topic usually covered in their biographies, although Cook's scholarly biographer, J.C. Beaglehole, makes one wonder during his account of the customary naval diet of the eighteenth century when he mentions 'the hard-baked biscuit that yet was penetrable to every variety of noxious insect that haunted a ship'. Cook was an 'experimental eater' who tried dog in Tahiti, kangaroo in New South Wales and shags in New Zealand. He was prevented from sampling monkeys in Batavia when the tenderhearted Joseph Banks took mercy on half a dozen which had been tethered and were waiting to be killed. Banks cut the rope.

Neither does seasickness rate a mention in sailing manuals, even when they have such comprehensive titles as the *Complete Sailing Handbook* and *The Yachtsman's A–Z*. Always a model of honesty, Dame Naomi James, who officially launched the *Spirit of New Zealand*, is one of the few famous sailors prepared to mention in print her bouts with nausea.

In 1980, she competed in the *Observer* Single-Handed Trans-Atlantic Race (usually

Top: *There are times when cabin bread is the only thing you can bear to eat!* (Alfred Memelink)

Above: *Whatever possessed us to sign on for this voyage?* (Alfred Memelink)

Seasick trainees are harnessed to the leeward side of the ship — in this case, the port side during SOA voyage 465 from Auckland to Gisborne. The two talking in the foreground seem to be recovering well! (Caroline Ramsay)

abbreviated to the OSTAR) in her yacht *Kriter Lady*. Towards the end of the event, as she was nearing Rhode Island, she spent a miserable day plagued with a severe headache. Because the wind kept changing, she was forced to stay on deck for hours making adjustments to the mainsail, genoa and storm jib. 'At last, feeling weak and shaky,' she reported a year later in her splendid volume of memoirs, *At Sea On Land*, 'I got below, made some toast and baked beans which I forced down. It didn't stay down for long, so I resorted to two paracetamol and two seasickness tablets and returned to my bunk. I tried to relax so the tablets could work, but the motion was becoming violent. Every now and then, just as I was dropping off to sleep, *Kriter Lady* would leap through a wave crest leaving my stomach suspended as she fell to the bottom. Putting in the last reef and winching it home finished me off completely; I was ill for a long time before I crawled shakily back to my bunk.'

Seasickness has no favourites. It doesn't pay to boast about one's constitution too soon, for anyone can be afflicted, even a brilliant sailor like Dame Naomi. Great strapping six-footers can suddenly succumb while puny-looking teenagers turn out to have cast-iron stomachs. When you're about to be sick, nothing else in the world matters. You don't want company (and especially not the company of strangers). You don't care how spectacular the view around you is. Competitions are no longer of any consequence. The intricacies of sail theory are definitely of no interest. All you want is for the internal turmoil to end.

Karla Hill from Taumarunui High School sailed on the *Spirit of Adventure* in March

Trainees on SONZ voyage 173 work hard at the capstan to raise the anchor, about 20 metres down, at Harataonga Bay, Great Barrier Island.

1993. She reported to the *Ruapehu Press* afterwards, 'Even though I was sick for the first three days, so was everyone else, except two people, and we still had to carry out our duties.'

Even before her voyage in the *Spirit of Adventure* in September 1992, Serean Adams was used to sailing on her father's yacht. Nevertheless she told the *Hibiscus Coaster*, 'It took us all a couple of days to get our sea-legs and even I got a bit seasick in the rough seas and gale-force winds. This was after boasting that I never got seasick and then being sent to the wheelhouse to act as navigator—the place where you're most likely to get sick.'

Robert Searle from Gisborne told the *Eastland Sun* early in 1993, 'At one stage, most people were throwing up, including even some of the crew, and the chef wasn't feeling too good either. It turned out I was the only one who could handle being below in the galley, so

Top: *Trainees on SONZ voyage 149 from Bluff to Lyttelton weave baggywrinkles, used to prevent chafing on the sails, from rope yarn.*

Above: *A baggywrinkle factory at work on SONZ voyage 97 at Port Underwood, in the Marlborough Sounds.* (Donna MacIntosh)

Still harnessed, but beginning to recover from seasickness on SOA voyage 389.

(Greg Walker)

cooked—and I was quite disappointed when not many people seemed interested in the food.'

I particularly admire the understatement of Katherine Fippard from Tauhara College, who talked to the *Taupo Times* about the first two days of her voyage on the *Spirit of New Zealand* from Lyttelton to Wellington in March 1993. 'I was lucky enough to be sick only 14 times.'

Although seasickness is anything but a joke while you're suffering from it, the best way for the trainees to recover their dignity afterwards is by keeping their sense of humour and joining in the general laughter. Trainees are usually reminded early in the voyage of the advantages of chundering to leeward rather than windward. Since the mid-seventies, a Chunderthon Trophy has been awarded at the end of each voyage, with contestants judged 'on quantity, style, distance, colour, texture, velocity and courtesy towards where it's deposited'.

Teenage constitutions are remarkably resilient. Trainees can groan through one day, harnessed to the rail in their banana skins, 'depositing' frequently over the side, and then recover their appetite the next—and not just an appetite for chicken salad or roast lamb and vegetables or custard and apricot pie.

Because there are so many different palates to cater for, the cooks generally avoid anything too fancy and keep the food fairly simple. Usually they will prepare bacon, eggs, toast and cereal for breakfast; soup and sandwiches for lunch; and a casserole, spaghetti dish or a

The daily chores include scrubbing spuds (top) *and de-seeding pumpkins* (above).
(Alfred Memelink)

Boys will be boys! (Alfred Memelink)

roast for dinner, with bread and butter pudding, a fruit tart or apple crumble for dessert.

'We spent most of day two and three getting to know each other, learning how to work together as a team and also sailing in 56-knot winds around Kawau Island,' 17-year-old Raewyn Scott from Stanmore Bay told the *Hibiscus Coaster* in September 1992. 'By day four we were all having a great time.'

The mood of most trainees brightens around the fourth or fifth day. Charlotte Gardner from Cambridge was one of the sixth-formers aboard the *Spirit of New Zealand* on a voyage from Lyttelton to Wellington in April 1993. 'By the time day five had passed,' she reported in the *Cambridge Independent*, 'the 40-trainee crew were beginning to reap the rewards of the hard work and dedication over the previous week. The day was glorious, and there was no better feeling than gliding through the Marlborough Sounds in full sail and at full speed with four dolphins swimming alongside. Also, by this point in the voyage, lifelong friendships had been built.'

Chapter Seven:
The Middle of the Journey

Life aboard the *Spirit* ships is busy from sunrise to lights out. The normal routine is to have lunch about noon (or 1200 hours on the 24-hour clock), dinner about 1800 hours and teabreaks at 1045 and 1445. Usually the trainees decide themselves, in consultation with the master or first mate, when lights out will be. Those not on night duty are usually in their bunks by 2100 hours, although sometimes the time is extended for socialising. There are seldom any complaints about going to bed too early. The trainees are usually exhausted, glad to sleep and resentful of anybody in their dormitories who feels compelled to talk.

During the day, tending the sails is the first priority. Or to use nautical terminology, making, reefing and furling the sails. Reefing is the process of shortening the surface area of sails during high winds. At first most of the trainees don't have a clue about sails. Or perhaps I should say they don't have a clew (the lower after corner). Gradually, however, they become more familiar. As well as distinguishing the clew from the tack (the lower fore corner), they learn to tell the leech (the edge away from the mast) from the luff (the edge next to the mast or stay). They learn the names of the various sails.

A sizable proportion of each day, one might say, is spent bending. This doesn't just mean that the trainees' bodies are forced into a series of angles and curves. Bending is a general sea term for fastening anything. Thus one bends halyards and sheets on to sails and bends sails on to masts and stays.

As well as the regular business of tending the sails, preparing meals and keeping the ship clean, there are safety drills and lectures, usually conducted by the master or first mate. 'We had three drills that we had to practise,' Serean Adams from Red Beach recalls, 'fire and collision, man overboard and abandon ship. In our man overboard drill, it took us ten minutes to get back to our pretend victim—a buoy—and we were all thankful that one of us hadn't been sent overboard.'

An unfortunate misprint in the *Southland Times* on 8 August 1987, midway through a former trainee's report, led to an entirely erroneous impression of cruelty: 'All of a sudden one of the officers threw a boy overboard and shouted Man Overboard!' Actually the thrown object was not a male trainee but a buoy.

Every trainee has a turn at the wheel, getting the feel of a ship under way, and her reaction to wheel movements. Usually they begin with just a short spell, but then a longer period which includes the use of the compass. The common tendency is to overdrive.

Opposite: *Lowering the* Spirit of Adventure*'s sails as she enters Goldsworthy Bay, near Kawau Island.* **(Alfred Memelink)**

A rather seasick-looking bunch gathers around the helm on SOA voyage 465 from Auckland to Gisborne. (Caroline Ramsay)

Chartwork is an important component of any ten-day voyage. Together a pair of trainees, Emma Pond and Daniel George, from SONZ voyage 97, plot a course along Banks Peninsula. (Donna MacIntosh)

Gathered around the chart table, trainees on SONZ voyage 173 attend to words of wisdom from the master, Bill Curry.

There are also stints in the engine room and the wheelhouse. When the ship is moving, there needs to be someone on the bowsprit to watch for small vessels crossing in front of the ship and report these back to the helm.

There's also chartwork, beginning with the recognition of such common features as shorelines, rocks, lighthouses, currents, prominent shore features. And there's the learning of navigation skills, such as how to fix the ship's position by taking two or more bearings, working with deviation tables, learning the difference between true and magnetic north, and the ship's compass bearings and the need to correct compass errors.

The officers recognise the importance of allowing some time for fun. In good weather, there could be an afternoon swim. Or a rope (popularly known as a Tarzan rope) might be dangled from the yard so that trainees can have an exhilarating swing along the outside of the ship before plunging into the sea. There might be a contest for dropping an egg in a parachute from the yard down to the deck. There might even be time for sunbathing.

'Trainees should be occupied at all times on interesting and diverse activities, which at times stretch their limits of physical and mental stamina, and instruction of a good quality should always be available to them. This however must be balanced with time for relaxing, enjoyment—pure "fun" activity,' says the *Instructor's Handbook*.

Mast-climbing might qualify as both fun and a challenge too. There are times when it's necessary to go aloft and stand out on the foot ropes of the yard to reef or furl the topsail. But a lot of the time the trainees go aloft for the thrill of it or because they want to overcome their fear. Arguably the world record for the most people on a mast at one time was set by 55 youngsters on the *Spirit of New Zealand* in Wellington Harbour in 1992.

'During a voyage early in 1981, from Lyttelton via Stewart Island and Bluff to Dunedin, I was aboard as deck officer,' the trust's chairman Stephen Fisher recalls. 'There was one trainee who was the largest and most uncoordinated of the team. Although prone to sea-sickness and notably lacking in self-confidence, he was also as keen as mustard and had practised his knots to such an extent he could tie them all behind his back more quickly than any of the others could tie them in front.

'Time and time again he would don his safety harness and hurry forward with the others to climb aloft. But each time his courage failed him. He would place his hands on the shrouds, and one foot on the rail, but the other foot never quite left the deck.

'On the tenth and final day as we sailed into calm waters after experiencing the rigours of Foveaux Strait, the beauty of Stewart Island and the albatross colony of Taiaroa Head, with the berth in sight, he climbed the rigging for the first time.'

In the words of one of the other volunteer officers on that voyage, John

A rowing team gets off to a wet start during SOA voyage 419 from Napier to Nelson in January 1992. (Greg Walker)

Top: *Races in the whalers and inflatables are a feature of most voyages. These trainees on SOA voyage 465 from Auckland to Gisborne are obviously enjoying the unscheduled swim.* (Caroline Ramsay)

Above: *The beginning of a boat race.* (Alfred Memelink)

McKenzie (a trustee from 1972 until his death in March 1989): 'As we quietly motored up the river from Port Chalmers to Dunedin we were all astounded to see him confidently clinging to the upper yard with a grin from ear to ear. There was not a trainee or crew member who did not have a tear in his eye as we applauded from the deck below.'

Every effort is made to include at least one night sail in the ten-day programme, since this really puts the trainees on their mettle. When the ship isn't moving, evenings aboard can seem quite long, particularly in winter. There might be a de-brief session on the day's activities when trainees can ask questions, points can be explained and the following day's pro-gramme discussed. Alternatively, the trainees might watch videos on sailing. Quizzes, pitching one watch against an-other, are a good method of establishing how much or, alas, how little has been learned during the day. The captain or the mates might also address the trainees in a formal lecture, although it would be hard to gainsay the wisdom of a note in the *Instructor's Handbook*: 'the more interesting formal lectures can quite satisfactorily be given in the evenings, but these will not be well received after a long hard day, or if not delivered in a brisk and imaginative way.'

It's not all work and no play: swinging from the lower yard is always a popular way to go for a swim. (Alfred Memelink)

Tastes differ, of course, as do levels of concentration. It's impossible to please everyone. In its September 1988 issue, the trust's quarterly magazine featured a report on a weekend voyage from Marsden Wharf to Motuihe and Waiheke Islands for 55 young people 'at risk', selected with the assistance of the Auckland Citizens' Youth Resource Centre, Tamaki College Community Programme, Onehunga Boxing Club, Auckland City Mission and Youthtown. Comments were included from the youngsters, identified by first names only. A young fellow named Nat voiced his opinion of the evening's entertainment. 'The video on sailing was stink and should have been thrown overboard.'

Since one of the trust's larger aims is to foster self-confidence, the trainees are gently en-couraged in the art of public speaking. So in the evening they might each be asked for a one-minute talk. There might be round robins where goals and expectations are discussed. The trainees might debate the qualities that go towards making a good leader. They might even role-play a job interview situation. 'On our third day,' Serean Adams recalls, 'we had a big "introductions" night in which we introduced who we were, our interests and sports and what we hoped to achieve on our voyage. I was the last trainee to speak which was a bit annoying because by then everyone was tired and just wanted to go to bed.'

The officers recognise that about midway through the voyage comes a longing for land. An attempt is usually made on day six to have some shore leave. New Zealand abounds in offshore islands and these, rather than the mainland, are the usual destinations for shore leave, although Coromandel Peninsula is also popular. It's a kind of freedom to be able to stretch your legs and swing your arms. There could be a bush walk, such as a six-hour climb to the summit of Mt Hobson on Great Barrier Island. Mt Hobson is only 621 metres high, but it's a rugged climb through mainly manuka and kanuka scrub.

When the ship is anchored, the trainees might learn how to rig a small sailing dinghy. Or there might be interwatch races in the whalers and rubber dinghies. Rowing comes naturally to some people, but not to many. Few trainees could match the feat of Colin

Quincey, one of the *Spirit of Adventure*'s former masters, who rowed across the Tasman Sea against the prevailing winds and currents in February 1977 in his 6-metre flat-bottomed dory *Tasman Tres-passer* (now on display in Hobson Wharf, the Auckland Maritime Museum). He left from the Hokianga Harbour and made landfall at Marcus Bay (about 190 kilometres north of Brisbane) 63 days and 1215 nautical miles later. After landing, he had to walk a kilometre before he found a house. Then he had to brave the response when he said, 'Hello, I've just rowed over from New Zealand.'

Ashore, equipped with an axe, a knife, a rope, life jackets, sailcloth and one oar, the trainees might build a survival raft using loose timber (no growing timber to be touched) or build a more substantial raft with a sail and steering facility capable of carrying six people back to the ship. Or they could erect a flagpole of sufficient size to fly a flag about a metre or so above the ground. They might have a tug-of-war on the beach, or relay races. In the evening, there might be a barbecue on the beach and a singalong around a camp fire. Part of the day could be spent gathering firewood. With conservation in mind, part of the trainees' shore leave usually involves tidying up the beach. They might even have a sandfly-killing contest. The record is 300 sandflies in ten minutes at Preservation Inlet in the far south in February 1987.

The trainees also have a chance to try their hand at mapwork ashore with some orienteering. 'A good map can be as absorbing as a well-written novel,' says English expert John Disley in his book *Tackle Orienteering*. In theory the same rules of navigation ought to hold good on land as at sea. In practice, distance can be very hard to estimate in the bush with the light and visibility changing quickly. Relating what you see on the map to what you see around you is not easy. Tempers tend to be at their worst when the trainees are already weary and they have the impression that someone else from their watch (or elsewhere on the ship) is leading them along the wrong path. Thus orienteering can be a fairly stringent test of newly formed friendships.

If there are any shops, the trainees will assuredly visit them and buy up all the available chocolate and soft drinks. To the small stores at places like Port Fitzroy (on Great Barrier Island) or Oban (on Stewart Island), the *Spirits* are a godsend, particularly in winter, when business is otherwise lean. While black market activities are rare among the trainees, there are tales nevertheless of chocolate bars changing hands for seven or eight times their normal value during the shipbound days.

If there are any waterfalls within easy distance of the shore they will be popular with female trainees desperate to wash their hair properly after five or six days of nothing but salt water. Hot springs are also popular after the dawn swims. There was a memorable occasion, however, a few years ago when the *Spirit of Adventure* was anchored at Whangaparapara Bay on Great Barrier Island. A group of girls tramped to the hot water springs for a long-awaited bath. They later discovered, much to their embarrassment, that they had bathed in the middle of an army manoeuvre. They had been surrounded throughout by men in camouflage gear hiding in the bush.

'Simply by sailing in a new direction
You could enlarge the world.'
(*Allen Curnow*, Landfall in Unknown Seas)

Chapter Eight:
Taking Over

On 17 January 1975, the New Zealand ensign on the *Spirit of Adventure* was suddenly replaced with the skull and crossbones. Dressed as pirates, a fierce-looking all-girl crew made Captain Pony More walk the plank. This was not a full-fledged mutiny, however, but just a playful way of farewelling Pony who was retiring that day from his position as the ship's permanent master. On a friendlier note, the girls also presented him with a chocolate cake.

There have been many other occasions when the trainees have taken over the ship. These have not been mutinies, but a crucial part of the democratic process.

When I was at university I remember one of my lecturers, Wystan Curnow, saying that the aim of a good education should be to render the teacher redundant. At the end of a successful course you ought to be able to go off on your own without needing the teacher's help. Wystan works in the English Department, but his dictum holds good whether the subject is accountancy, civil engineering, medicine, music, karate or sailing.

Wystan's father is the poet Allen Curnow. Fifty years ago, to mark the centenary of the Treaty of Waitangi, Allen wrote a poem, 'Landfall in Unknown Seas', which deals, in part, with the experiences of pioneer sailors. It begins, 'Simply by sailing in a new direction/You could enlarge the world.'

Trainees must have a similar sense of exhilaration, mingled, of course, with anxiety, when they take over control. Mind you, the aim is not so much to discover a new direction as to keep the ship on course for its port of destination. The trainee captain is allowed a brief conference with the permanent master early on Thursday morning.

'Once a trainee has been given a task, keep out of the way as much as possible, giving ample opportunity to sort out any problems . . . before assisting,' says the *Instructor's Handbook*. Later it adds, 'Trainees must receive sufficient training, experience and guidance to be able to achieve particular tasks WITHOUT DIRECT SUPERVISION, for until this stage is reached there does not exist a situation where leadership, initiative and self-confidence have room to develop.'

The ultimate task for the trainees is to sail the ship on their own. They are given a chance to do so on the last full day of each voyage. This is a tradition which goes back to the earliest voyages.

There have been occasions when the permanent officers felt that the group of trainees under their supervision simply weren't up to scratch and thus decided not to hand over the

Opposite: *After several ship-bound days at the start of a ten-day voyage, an excursion in a whaler gives the trainees a chance to view the* Spirit of New Zealand *from the outside.*

95

As part of the safety programme, the Spirit of New Zealand *participates in a simulated rescue by the Auckland-based Westpac rescue helicopter on Waitemata Harbour. That's a dummy on the stretcher, not a stricken trainee!*

ship to their care, but these have been few and far between. By and large, the trainees are highly motivated. They applied to be aboard the *Spirits* in the first place; they weren't coerced. They want their voyage to be a success and sailing by themselves is the final trial. They might be apprehensive, even scared, but they're keen to prove themselves.

The ten-day voyages usually end on a Friday morning. The trainees take command of the ship on Thursday. On Wednesday night they gather in the great cabin of the *Spirit of Adventure* or the aft cabin of the *Spirit of New Zealand* to elect their own crew, including a captain, first mate, navigators, engineers, cooks and watch officers.

Do boys vote for boys and girls for girls? Do the best-looking youngsters win all the votes? Sometimes. Voting motives are seldom pure. By and large, however, the trainees are very fair in their assessments. They almost always accept that the election is a serious business. Skylarking on this occasion is very rare. Clowns are seldom voted in. The trainees realise, after all, that if they put a practical joker in charge of the galley, they will be obliged to eat the results. If they vote someone who is hopeless at geography and arithmetic as the navigators, they will have to work extra hard to correct the mistakes if they want to catch the planes and trains the following day.

Bigheads tend to get their comeuppance. Those who came on board bragging that they knew everything already because their parents own large yachts have probably sickened

96

A special cake commemorates SOA voyage 360 around the Hauraki Gulf.

(Alfred Memelink)

everyone off. Over the previous nine days the trainees have been watching one another carefully. Real knowledge has had plenty of time to be tested.

In all probability they know even better than the permanent officers which of their number can be trusted to get the job done. The elections aren't just popularity contests. It's not unusual for the trainees to decide that people still lacking a little in confidence should be given a chance to prove their mettle.

The election is a lesson in maturity. It teaches the trainees democracy at work. Winners are taught the meaning of responsibility and losers have to bear their defeat graciously. Not every trainee has the opportunity to become an officer for a day. Some of the young people are simply passed over. The democratic system might be the best political system, but it's not without its share of pain. But as the popular adage says, there's no gain without pain.

The permanent officers have their own opinions, of course, on which trainees are best suited to which jobs, but they hold their tongues. They do not overrule the trainees' decisions by saying, 'Oh no, you're not putting him in charge. He's a vandal and an idiot. Make her the captain instead.'

In most nations, there's a transition period, lasting weeks or even months, before the elected president takes over from the incumbent. The process is much faster on the *Spirit* ships. Trainee captains assume their duties directly after being voted in. In fact, it's their responsibility to supervise the election of other officers.

Opposite and above: *Given a few simple materials, can you parachute an egg safely from the top of the main mast to the deck? Here, trainees on SONZ voyage 173 test their skill.*

Launching the whalers from the **Spirit of New Zealand.**

The first ever trainee captain on the *Spirit of New Zealand* was Angela Gooch, who was a sixth former at Heretaunga College at the time. She wrote an essay about her experiences which was published in the December 1986 issue of the trust's quarterly magazine, *The Spirit*. 'Something I was worried about,' Angela confided, 'was that because I was small and female, people wouldn't listen to me, but that wasn't the case at all. It was a team effort, with everyone putting forward their ideas about what should happen next, and it was because of everyone's contributions that we were successfully able to sail the boat from Mahurangi Heads to Rangitoto Island.'

Serean Adams was elected captain on a *Spirit of Adventure* voyage in September 1992. 'Being captain was a lot of fun but for a first time it was also very stressful,' she said later. 'I had to run the elections for the crew positions such as first mate, navigators and so forth, and I also had to write up night orders which people on night watch had to follow. These were things like bearings, depth and angle and what to do if they altered dramatically.

'The next day saw us with sails set okay but getting nowhere. It took us a while to figure out that the navigators had plotted a course too high up wind and that we'd have to come down a little if we wanted to get anywhere. Another problem we had was getting too close to the rocks off Rangitoto Island. Knowing we had to stay one nautical mile away from any rocks we were dismayed to find our navigators had put us within 0.7 nautical miles of underwater rocks off the island. I immediately ordered 'all hands on deck' and as soon as everyone was up we tacked.'

If you can sail a whaler successfully, you ought to be able to sail anything.

While it's probably fair to say the main strain is borne by the trainee captain, it would be a mistake to think that the other trainee officers get off lightly. On a voyage on the *Spirit of Adventure* from Gisborne to Auckland in April 1993, Bernadette Ross, a seventh former at Opunake High School, was elected cook. 'It was a pretty long day,' she said afterwards. 'My assistant and I had to prepare and cook three meals for 34 people.'

In addition to the general problems of navigation and deciding which sails are best suited to the wind conditions, every part of the New Zealand coastline has its unique difficulties. One of the difficulties in the Waitemata Harbour and the inner Hauraki Gulf is that so many Aucklanders are fond of sailing. On a fine day, vessels of every shape and size take to the water. Thus the trainees might have to cope with traffic congestion. They might even encounter a yacht race. The trainees often concede that it's good to see the real captain back at the helm at the end of the day.

On the last night, there is a prizegiving ceremony. Some of the awards, such as the Jewellers' Award for the most improved trainee, are serious. Others are just fun. The Boots Award, for example, is a little pair of baby's gumboots presented for the most unnautical thing done on board. Usually this goes to the most stupid accident outside of sailing.

Serean Adams recalled some of the prizes on her voyage for the *Hibiscus Coaster*. 'The Non-nautical Booboo Award went to Kim, who had leaned over the stove and caught her jumper on fire—without realising she was ablaze. The Bruises Award went to Polly for falling down the stairs the most times and giving everyone else bruises by standing on their hands and feet.'

Opposite: *Mate Deanna Douglas supervises as the* Lady Hamilton *is pulled ashore on* **Great Barrier Island.**

Above: *The* **Lady Hamilton** *and the* **Lord Nelson** *returning to the* **Spirit of New Zealand.**

Bernadette Ross recalls that there was much competition for the Chunderthon Trophy on her voyage, but the girl who eventually won 'aimed with great accuracy from a top bunk at 4.30 a.m.'

There's a prize for all the trainees on the last night. They are allowed a one-minute hot shower each. This is greeted with great elation, especially by those lucky enough to be among the first in line.

The next morning when the ship puts into the wharf, there are tearful farewells. The trainees pose for final photographs. They promise to stay in contact with one another. Needless to say, some will be more diligent than others about keeping these promises, but they are all sincerely meant at the time. Some trainees don't want to leave. Fiona Dawson from Queen Charlotte College was part of a ten-day voyage around Pelorus Sound on the *Spirit of New Zealand* in May 1992. 'I still wish I was on the ship,' she told the *Picton Paper* a month later. For others the emotions are mixed. They don't want to part from their new friends, but they're also keen to get home to their old friends and their families. 'Being on the *Spirit of Adventure* made me really appreciate life at home,' Natasha Jones said. This is a double-edged comment. The comforts of home life become apparent only after they are removed.

(Auckland Star)

Heather Green, from Newlands College in Wellington, was on a voyage in May 1992 from Picton to Wellington. 'The day before I left I was sitting here at home crying and not wanting to go, and at the end of the voyage I left the boat in tears.' That's a typical reaction, although gender differences are still such that the girls tend to weep openly as they hug one another goodbye, whereas the boys just dab surreptitiously at their eyes.

There are rituals of parting. Often there's a mass exodus to the nearest McDonald's, KFC or Georgie Pie. After ten days of healthy eating (bar the chocolate), the trainees begin to miss junk food and yield to the desire to 'pig out on grease'. But there's a social reason for this, as well as a dietary one. There are boats and trains and planes to catch home, but a shared hamburger meal and chips can be a way of prolonging friendships for another hour or two. Will the promises to write be honoured? Time and distance often get in the way of good intentions. Some of the trainees will join the Voyagers Club and sail on the *Spirits* again as leading hands. When they cross the gangway at the end of the voyage, there's a marked difference in their stride from the first hesitant steps they took less than a fortnight earlier. Over the last ten days most of the trainees have changed and they know it. There's a new confidence in the way they walk, the way they hold themselves.

Previous page: *The* Spirit of New Zealand *about to tack as she approaches Barretts Reef on a wild day in Wellington Harbour.* (Alfred Memelink)

106

Chapter Nine:
Crewing on the 'Spirits'

In the 21 years since the launch of STS *Spirit of Adventure*, over 20,000 youth trainees have taken part in the trust's youth development programme, and a total of over 50,000 trainees have sailed on the two *Spirit* ships. This is an impressive testimony to Lou Fisher's vision in establishing a sail training programme in New Zealand, and to the dedication of the many people who have been involved with The Spirit of Adventure Trust in the intervening years. Among those who have been central to the success of the Spirit programme are the full-time and volunteer crew; and it is an indication of the programme's effectiveness that many ex-trainees now retain their connection with the trust in this capacity.

In June 1994 I chatted to two of the longest-serving permanent crew members, Paul Leppington and Steve Gamble, about their work; while Tessa Duder spoke to Wellington-based volunteer Graham Weakley, and Rosemary Parkin who served as a mate in the mid-1980s.

Finding the Right Mix:
Senior Master Paul Leppington

'It's a successful voyage if the trainees have a good time and learn something about themselves,' says Paul Leppington. 'It doesn't matter much whether they learn to sail. The weather isn't important either. It's possible to have a great voyage in pouring rain. From the crew's perspective, you might have to work a bit harder against the weather on a voyage based in Wellington Harbour or Lyttelton Harbour than you would on a voyage around the Hauraki Gulf, but the trainees won't be aware of that. From their point of view, everything's new and exciting, wherever the voyage is taking place and whether it's summer or winter.

'The attitude of the crew is crucial right from Day One. The trust is careful about the people selected as permanent officers on the ships. They need to have the right mix of nautical and life skills. They're in a sailing environment, but they're working on a youth development programme. I always tell prospective crew members, "If you're in love with sailing ships, but you can't stand young people, then don't sail with us. There are plenty of other boats around that you can sail on." The trust exists for the trainees' benefit and delight, not for the egos of the officers. That's the essential thing for the staff to get straight.

'I've seen a lot of voyages over the years and they've all been different. There are some constants, of course. There's always one really bolshy trainee on every voyage, and somebody with an outstandingly sunny nature by way of balance. But because the people, the

107

Senior master Paul Leppington first joined The Spirit of Adventure Trust as a mate in 1975.

place, the weather and the circumstances keep changing, each voyage is a unique experience. The input from the volunteer crew adds a fresh dimension to every voyage. I've met some marvellous people through the volunteer organisation and I've learned a lot about sailing from them. But I've learned a lot from the trainees too. They often come up with novel solutions to problems. They want to know the reasons why we hoist sails in a certain way. They ask questions about everything we do. Sometimes, in the course of the interrogative process, it becomes clear that there's actually a better way of getting a particular job done than the method we've traditionally used. The trainees aren't aware of the tradition. They come aboard with entirely fresh eyes.'

Born in Scarborough, Yorkshire, in 1943, Paul grew up close to the sea. Swimming, fishing, boating and raft-building were all part of his childhood. For five years, beginning at the age of 11, he studied full-time at Graham Sea Training and Engineering School, a private nautical school for naval cadets. One of his hobbies there was restoring the collection of model ships. During his fourth year, he was selected as a trainee on the *Sir Winston Churchill*, the three-masted topsail schooner run by Britain's Sail Training Association.

After he finished his secondary education, Paul's seafaring career took him to many parts of the world, including New Zealand. While he was in Auckland in 1975, he spied an advertisement in the *New Zealand Herald* for a second mate on the *Spirit of Adventure*.

'I hadn't even seen the ship when I applied for the job,' he recalls. 'I first sailed on the *Spirit of Adventure* on voyage 27 in April 1975. Stan Hulford was in command. Even though I'd been on a sail training ship as a cadet, it was a pretty steep learning curve for me. I didn't have much confidence at the time when it came to addressing groups of people. I had to develop some presentation skills.'

Paul has been associated with the trust in one capacity or another since 1975, but he has not been employed continuously throughout that period as a permanent crew member. 'I think it's a good idea to take a break every couple of years and do something different,' he says. 'That way you come back fresh and committed. Otherwise you tend to burn out, because you have to put a lot of energy into every voyage. I'm married with a young son. It's hard for married crew to be away from home for long stretches, doing ten-day voyages

Paul Leppington, captain on the Spirit of New Zealand*'s first southern voyage in January 1987, shooting with a sextant off Banks Peninsula.* (John Duder)

more or less back-to-back. It was largely for the sake of family life that I first went ashore and set up a rigging business.'

In 1983 Paul helped design and build the replica of HMS *Bounty* which was used in the Roger Donaldson film *The Bounty*, starring Mel Gibson as Fletcher Christian and Anthony Hopkins as Captain Bligh. Paul was also the skipper who sailed the replica to French Polynesia for the scenes filmed on location. Among the 18-strong crew on the journey from Whangarei to Tahiti was another future master of the *Spirits*, Steve Gamble. Both Paul and Steve can occasionally be glimpsed in the completed movie, suitably attired in eighteenth century costume. 'And with a lot more hair than we have now,' adds Paul.

Paul's current position as senior master with the trust is largely a shore-based, supervisory job, but he still participates in at least three or four ten-day voyages a year, as well as shorter officer-training voyages. 'I don't always go out as the captain,' he says. 'I might serve as one of the watch officers instead. Or I'll fill in for somebody who's sick or on leave. Nowadays my role is monitoring. I make sure that things are on the right track. Generally, I try not to interfere too much. I still really enjoy voyages on the *Spirits*.

'There are some differences between the two ships. Because she's smaller, the *Spirit of Adventure* is more intimate. You get to know the trainees quickly. There's not much that they're able to hide from you. With the *Spirit of New Zealand*, there's 40 trainees and 14 crew, so the captain probably has to work harder to motivate everybody and to counteract the tendency for large groups to become too formal and too fragmented. Young people are put off by too much formality. Both ships offer wonderful opportunities, but the group dynamics are different.

'One of the unofficial barometers I use to measure the success of any particular day aboard either ship is whether the trainees are starting to fall asleep around 8 p.m. (or 2000 hours). If they're still up and yahooing at night, there's something wrong. We're not challenging them enough or sucking enough energy out of them during the daytime. Mind you, the energy level of young people can be phenomenal. One lot recently went on a 22-kilometre hike from the east coast of Great Barrier Island to the top of Mount Hobson and back. When we returned to the ship, they were still rearing to go, so we did a night sail to Kawau Island. The crew members were exhausted at the end of that, but not the trainees. To pace the staff, so they can keep up with the young people's energy, we usually divide them into an A team and a B team.

'I run into former trainees all the time: it's always interesting to see how they're getting on. Because I've been involved with the trust for so long, some of the trainees I've known manage their own companies now. They're in their thirties and they have children older than my son. In fact, some of them have mentored me on the business of child-raising. Some of the people I remember as rather shy 15 or 16-year-olds are now successful lawyers, doctors and accountants. I tell the crew to enjoy talking to the trainees while they still can, because pretty soon it might cost them $170 or $180 for a consultation.

'I think it's a privilege to work with young people. They're bright and witty. They have their own opinions, but they're also looking for answers. The Spirit of Adventure Trust takes them away from their normal environment when they're at a formative stage in their lives, between the ages of 15 and 18, and gives them a chance to reflect, ask questions and expand their focus. I know the *Spirits* have a significant impact on a lot of people's lives. More often than not, something happens during a voyage which the trainees never forget. It might not be all that dramatic—just a subtle change in the way they look at themselves and the world around them.'

A Place in the Sun: Rosemary Parkin
by *Tessa Duder*

New Zealand in the early 1970s, at the beginning of the *Spirit* story, wasn't a great place for 'get-up-and-go' young women, even less for their mothers reared in the staid 1950s. The sixties had been a time of social upheaval, yet to be integrated into society; the new feminist wave, generated in the United States during that decade, had yet to gather strength in New Zealand.

It's probably fair to say that there wasn't much consideration of women, as trainees or officers, even less as masters or trustees, in the early deliberations to set up a sail training ship.

But times were changing, and women's voice for a place in the sun soon began to be heard. The good thing about the *Spirit* story is that there's little evidence of a pitched battle for participation and recognition; rather the reverse. The contribution of women in every aspect of the trust's work has grown steadily, encouraged rather than resisted. As one of the women who has grown with the organisation, I'm proud to be able to write that.

As evidence of this, voyages 11 and 13, the first girls' voyages in 1974, happened within

Captain Jennifer Roberts, who became the trust's first female master in 1982, with Captain Nick Hylton, senior master from 1979 to 1992. (Gisborne Herald)

six months of voyage 1, which was assumed to be only for boys; and on those girls' trips, the first female watch officers were among the crew. Five years later, former trainee Heidi Richardson became the first woman to be employed as a mate.

In 1982, Captain Jennifer Roberts became the first female master, Captain Margaret Pidgeon the second in 1985. Girls' voyages acquired parity on the *Spirit of Adventure* quite early on, and the *Spirit of New Zealand* was designed and built to take equal numbers of male and female trainees.

The trust has long had a policy of employing female mates. It's been taken as read that women are rostered as volunteer crew, up to and including first mate, appropriate to their qualifications and experience. There have been many female cooks, and even a handful of totally female voyages, but as yet, no female employed as engineer. In 1986 it was a team of women who stowed extra pig-iron ballast in the bilges of the newly commissioned *Spirit of New Zealand*, and an unpleasant job it was, too. In the mid-nineties, curiously, there are significantly more girls than boys wanting the *Spirit* experience.

Quite a few of the older female hands would agree with former first mate, Rosemary Parkin, that much of the credit for the trust's pro-active stance on female crew should go to Nick Hylton, senior master from 1979 until his retirement in 1992. I remember once challenging Nick that of course the blokes liked all-male voyages best. He would have none of it, nor would he be goaded by interviewers into saying whether boys' or girls' trips, or male or female trainees, were 'best'. Everyone had something to offer, he would say firmly.

Rosemary Parkin, however, did echo something of my own experience when she told me that it was not all plain sailing during her years as a female mate on a sailing ship.

I asked her how macho teenage boys reacted to having a female watch officer. That, it appeared, was less of a problem than working out a relationship with male volunteer crew, older men who sailed as third or fourth mates. Even capable young women with the kind of experience and natural air of authority of Rosemary still had to prove themselves, it seems, to be not only as good as, but better than their male counterparts. While the trainees soon accepted her, some of the male volunteers took longer.

'My style concentrates on working together to achieve a result. I like to spend time establishing a relationship, then getting results. I concentrated on the teaching—I tended to be less sympathetic than some to seasick trainees. I used to say to them, you'll be okay. But no, I didn't see myself as a role model especially. Teamwork and outcomes are important to me.'

The outcome of Rosemary's ten years' experience with the *Spirit* is now the new position of small boat inspector for the Maritime Safety Authority, covering a patch from Taupo to North Cape. Wakas, kayaks, dinghies, pleasure boats—she's responsible for everything that floats except fishing boats, and for much legal assessment and education of commercial and pleasure boat operators as well. She was appointed to the position in April 1994 and says she is inventing her job as she goes along. She's the only woman in the Maritime Safety Authority, one of the three transport divisions accountable to the Minister of Transport, at her level of responsibility.

'I tend to be held up as an example,' she says, although she disclaims any suggestion of a feminist label: 'I'm more interested in getting the job done than in scoring points for anyone.'

Rosemary came from a Northland sailing family, crewing a variety of small yachts during her teenage years with her brothers and friends. In November 1980 she sailed on the *Spirit of Adventure* on a five-day post-refit voyage for Duke of Edinburgh award candidates.

'It was a funny trip, with Guide leaders and lots of us who'd just been accredited UE. There was a girl who'd got 99 for School C. maths—I'd got 90 and thought that was pretty good! The oldest was 28. We didn't do much sailing, though there was one long passage from Coromandel to Kawau which I loved. We did a lot of work on the rigging. I went

Rosemary Parkin, now small boat inspector for the Maritime Safety Authority, first sailed on the Spirit of Adventure *in 1980.*

home with rescue steel all over my clothes.'

Rosemary never did a ten-day trip as a trainee. Her school, Whangaroa College in Northland, 'thought I was too well rewarded already'. But in August 1981, now a student at teachers' college, she sailed as a leading hand and so began a ten-year association with the *Spirit*.

Graduating from training college, and with a Boatmaster certificate collected along the way, Rosemary decided after five terms teaching maths and phys. ed. that the classroom was not for her.

So she clocked up nine months' sea-time on the Devonport ferries, sat her Commercial Launchmaster's ticket, and joined the *Spirit*'s paid crew at the end of 1986. The *Spirit of New Zealand* had been in commission only five months and the trust's administration was still feeling its way in its new role as a small shipping line.

By September 1988 it was time to move on, to more sea-going tickets and different experiences. In hindsight she recognises that the move was a good thing for her, but initially, as second mate on the *Bounty*, she ran into the old prejudices towards female crew: 'a relieving master who looked for my mistakes and basically didn't want me there'. By this time, however, she knew that she wanted to be a maritime professional and was prepared to slog her way through the difficult exams for Part A (Theory) of the Second Mate Foreign-Going ticket. 'I still don't have enough trading vessel sea-time,' she says. 'I'll finish it one day, given the opportunity.'

An impressive variety of nautical experiences now appears on Rosemary's CV. She took her first command in 1989, as skipper of the keelers run by the Auckland Harbour Cruise Company to give tourists match-racing experience on the Waitemata Harbour.

Then followed a spell as first mate on the barquentine *Soren Larsen* in the Pacific for the 1990 sesquicentennial celebrations; six months' laying cables, and later, as first mate on a dynamic positioning ship, surveying cables in Cook Strait; Pacific delivery cruises during 1991 and 1992 on two large private yachts; and a delivery voyage to Malaysia in 1993.

She returned to the *Spirit* paid crew for one further period, as first mate during the busy 1990 year when the two ships were involved in the sesquicentennial celebrations.

Now, however, in her early thirties and busy with her new job, she's keeping her options open for the future. Married to *Spirit* engineer Geoff Maurice in 1993, she doesn't necessarily see children in her future.

Chief executive of The Spirit of Adventure Trust, Bill McCook, sees her as a potential master, but Rosemary admits to no long-held and burning ambition to skipper a sailing ship for its own sake: 'I've gained a lot of experience sailing as first mate, and sailing as master would be a logical step in my professional development.' In the meantime, she is realistic about the unique demands of the position, in terms of a master's responsibility for the ship and the safety, welfare and education of its trainees.

The Making of a Volunteer: Graham Weakley
by Tessa Duder

At the end of 1992, the *Spirit of New Zealand* was in Wellington and 7000 scouts were in town for the thirteenth New Zealand international jamboree. Someone had the idea of giving them the taste of sailing before the mast.

Good idea, they said in the trust's Operations Office, seeing the opportunity for some serious fund-raising as well as good public relations. A ten-day voyage was cancelled, and responsibility for running a series of planned day sails was handed over to the trust's volunteer arm in Wellington, the Wellington Regional Association.

Enter two key Wellington figures: Adrienne Welch, the trust's national volunteer co-ordinator, appointed by the trust to represent the interests of its hundreds of volunteers nationwide. Adrienne, one of the trust's best-known volunteers through her previous work as advisor to the Voyagers Club, on this occasion headed the team handling the bookings, publicity and general administration.

The other was Graham Weakley, a quietly-spoken, 25-year-old computer expert, then vice-chairman of the Wellington Regional Association and himself a former Scout leader. In fact, it had originally been Graham's idea to give the Scouts a *Spirit* experience, and he undertook to handle the crewing.

For the 34 sailings, 3 a day over 12 days, the big, black, three-masted ship required a legal minimum of 13 crew per sailing. Allowing generous safety margins for totally 'green' passengers and Wellington's quixotic weather, even in high summer, Graham needed to roster around 20 crew each time the ship left the wharf.

'They did brilliantly,' says the then purser Pippa Tizzard. 'By getting volunteer crew from all over the country over that new year period, they gave the exercise a national flavour. Eighty-five scouts went out each time, but there were also sailings open to the holiday public, equally successful. It was a brilliant public relations exercise, and I have huge respect for Graham's work co-ordinating the crew. Not only that, but for everything he has done for the trust.'

After the last of those sailings, 1783 Scouts and over 100 volunteer crew had gone to sea, and the trust was $42,000 better off. Graham Weakley, as well he might, remembers the jamboree sailings as a highlight of his involvement with the regional association.

There are those of us who've known Graham from his early days with the organisation and hope that there will continue to be further highlights in the years to come.

Without that first experience as a trainee on voyage 243 in April 1984, Graham's life might have taken a completely different turn, and would very likely have had little or nothing to do with sailing or the sea. Although he's gone tramping since the age of ten and has climbed as a 'serious hobby' in the Mt Cook, Ruapehu and Kaikoura areas, there is no sailing background in his family whatsoever. As with Rosemary Parkin, Captain Nick Hylton comes up as having been influential on the shy 17-year-old.

'My first trip was from New Plymouth to Onehunga, via the Marlborough Sounds, with Nick as master,' says Graham. He had been selected by his school, St Patrick's College in Wellington, from 14 candidates who had expressed interest. The appeal was simply the chance of adventure.

'I almost dropped out twice,' he recalls. 'I'm a shy person. The thought of 32 total strangers was almost too much, but I made it to the wharf. I was elected navigator, and was one of two who gained their Safe Boating certificate. Now I think that the ability to work with strangers is one of the greatest things I've learnt through the *Spirit*.'

During that voyage the ship visited Anakiwa as guests of Outward Bound. 'The ropes course looked high at first, but it was easy after being aloft on *Spirit of Adventure*.'

Graham doesn't actually remember his first trip aloft: 'I'd been scared of heights, but not what you'd call terrified. The thing I really hated was being woken at 6 a.m. by the generator.' (I'll second that, as would many others. The key turns, the ship shudders into throbbing life; it's one rude awakening to be followed by another ten minutes later, the dreaded dawn swim). 'I trained myself to wake when I heard the engineer's footfalls. It wasn't so bad then.'

Graham Weakley, a mainstay of the trust's Wellington Regional Association and a skipper on the Wellington Harbour ferry, first sailed with the trust as a trainee in 1984.

He became a Voyager, and sailed as leading hand in 1985, and again the following year. In 1987 he did his first trip as one of four leading hands on the *Spirit of New Zealand*, again with Nick Hylton, who was clearly impressed with his competence and developing leadership skills: 'Nick told me never to come back on his ship as a leading hand.'

He took Nick's advice to move on, and has since sailed as a mate at every possible opportunity on ten-day trips, six-day trips, adult weekend and short sailings. He's now on his fifth record card, signed by the master at the conclusion of each voyage.

From a Safe Boating certificate, Graham made it via Boatmaster, Yachtmaster Coastal and a radar course to his Commercial Launch Master ticket in 1993. Being made redundant in 1991 from his computer job at National Mutual provided the incentive to clock up twelve months' sea-time on the Wellington Harbour ferry. For the next

Many trainees retain their association with the trust through the national Voyagers Club, which assigns the leading hands to each voyage, sends out a monthly newsletter and organises social activities. It is also responsible for providing buddies on voyages for young people with disabilities. Here members are practising a rescue drill at the 1986 Voyagers conference. (John Duder)

ticket, Coastal Master, considerably more sea-time is needed on commercial vessels. It's not, he says, a burning ambition.

A more attainable dream is to return to the STS *Leeuwin*, which operates out of Port Fremantle in Western Australia. In 1994 he sailed as a deck officer for three ten-day trips. This sister ship of the *Spirit of New Zealand*, says Graham, operates quite a different sort of training programme, largely because the rugged West Australian coastline compels the *Leeuwin* to spend most of each voyage at sea, with none of the shore activities enjoyed by *Spirit* trainees in the Hauraki Gulf, the Bay of Islands, the Marlborough Sounds and elsewhere. 'We, by comparison, are very strict about the going aloft routines. On the *Leeuwin* trainees can go up without an officer, although they do have to get permission. On the other hand, they are not allowed to set sail, even with a deck officer, without the bosun or mate supervising.'

He has hopes of a return visit in 1995, when the ship will voyage to Darwin and on to Indonesia. It would, he says, be great to be part of some sort of exchange.

Now working as a computer consultant, he's diffident about assessing the impact of the *Spirit* experience on his life, apart from the obvious and often-quoted things like helping a young person learn to cope with stress, to work under pressure, and to build up confidence in daily life. 'Before, I had a tendency to concentrate on my own task, not looking at the bigger picture. Now I think I do manage to turn around and look at the whole and see how I and my task fit in.'

As one who came up from the trainee ranks, he didn't have an adult baptism of fire: that first trip as a watch officer, which is no small ordeal for older volunteers. No matter how experienced they are on small boats and keelers, or even if they've been through the *Spirit*'s watch officer training course, nothing quite prepares first-time volunteers for the impact of a three-masted sailing ship or working with a watch of eager but bewildered trainees. He's rather glad he didn't go 'cold turkey', as an adult, commenting that 'it must be quite hard'. I can attest to that: my first voyage as watch officer, in 1981, was as steep a learning curve as that experienced by the trainees, combining in about equal measure exhilaration at tasks attempted and achieved with regular panic attacks at feeling inadequate. In middle-age, that can be quite a test.

For many volunteer crew, sailing as a deck officer is all they have the time or energy to contribute to the *Spirit* enterprise. Graham is one of a dedicated minority who've also involved themselves in the regional committee work, the politics, the fund-raising, the newsletters, the crew training nights, the rostering and the liaison work with the Auckland-based Operations Office.

He joined the Wellington Regional Association when it was first formed in 1988 and not long after became vice-chairman and eventually chairman. There's hardly a job on that committee Graham hasn't handled over the six years of his involvement. One particular area of interest was helping set up a new watch officer training programme, since taken up and developed in Auckland and nationally. Hours and hours of work went into that programme, says Graham.

Nor has he dodged the responsibility of representing the interests of the local volunteer association in working with the Operations Office. Occasionally tensions do develop, as is inevitable with any professional organisation that is so dependent on its volunteers and that operates nationally on a shoe-string. Despite the volatile, unpredictable nature of its ingredients—sailing ships and teenagers—the trust's tradition of good-will always prevails.

Adrienne Welch, particularly, has taken great personal pleasure in watching former trainees such as Graham develop as young, then mature adults, accepting responsible positions with the Voyagers Club and then the regional associations.

'He epitomises everything we like to see happen with the trainees. As chairman, he got things done, didn't just talk about them. And all his experience as a deck officer and committee person have given him the opportunity to learn skills he may not have had so relatively young.'

It was Graham's on-going loyalty, dedication and knowledge of the organisation—shared with others like him—that could allow the Operations Office the confidence to hand over the complete running of those 34 Christmas day sails to the regional volunteers. It was not without a few initial misgivings, given the very nature of an operation that combines sailing ships and teenagers, but they did it all the same. This faith in the loyalty and professional standards of its volunteers is one of the trust's characteristics most admired by overseas sail training organisations, and it is a credit to both.

From Trainee to Captain: Permanent Master Steve Gamble

When he first set foot on the *Spirit of Adventure* in March 1977, Steve Gamble was a raw 15-year-old from Edgewater College in Pakuranga, Auckland. 'As a matter of fact, I turned 15 on the voyage,' he recalls. 'I'm not sure how I got away with that. It would never happen nowadays. In my opinion, 15 is a bit young to get the full benefit of the *Spirit* experience, although as soon as I say that I can think of a few brilliant exceptions. I wasn't one of the exceptions, I'm afraid. I was young for my age. I didn't have the maturity to get the most out of my voyage. I know it was voyage 75 around the Hauraki Gulf, but to tell you the truth I'm hazy now about the details.'

All the same, Steve was inspired enough to become an active member of the Auckland branch of the Voyagers Club three years later. 'I loved the camaraderie of the Voyagers.

There was a good tight group of us in those days and we had a lot of fun. I think my love of sailing ships probably began with the Voyagers Club rather than my time as a trainee. I returned to the *Spirit of Adventure* eight times as a leading hand.'

After leaving school, Steve worked as a fireman in the Royal New Zealand Air Force. In 1983 he signed on as an able seaman and storekeeper on the replica of the *Bounty* during the filming of Roger Donaldson's remake of *The Bounty* in French Polynesia. When he returned to Auckland, he worked for a rigging company. In this capacity he helped build the rig for the *Spirit of New Zealand*. He joined the staff of The Spirit of Adventure Trust as a permanent mate in 1986.

'Apart from taking part in an ocean race to Japan and spending a month in Australia as part of an exchange programme with the sail training ship the *Leeuwin*, I worked continuously as a mate for four years. Probably that's a bit too long. Crew members need to sustain their enthusiasm in order to give the young people a fair deal, but the energy required is so intense that the burn-out rate is high. At the end of 1989 I joined a couple of other former *Spirit* employees, Alan and Derryn Wilson, on a large ocean yacht, *Freedom*, sailing around the world for three years. Of course, when I got back in 1992, I was keen to see what was happening with the trust.'

Steve became the first permanent master to have gone right through the ranks from trainee. 'My experience sailing as a mate under various captains has been invaluable to me,' he says. 'I picked up a great deal from all of them. In particular, I learned elegant and economical ways of getting jobs done. Paul Leppington taught me a lot about rigging, for example. I think it would be horribly daunting to come in cold and take command of either of the *Spirits*. I really respect people like Bill Curry who have done that. Me, I already knew the ships and some of the personnel pretty well by the time I became a captain.

'Every voyage is different, though. For one thing, the volunteer watch officers always bring in a new perspective. The two I had with me on my last voyage were just fantastic. Then there's the trainees themselves. They're not children. They're young adults. They're very intelligent and perceptive people. They think of wonderful ideas at times on how to sail the ship. I learn something new on every voyage. As a small instance, one lot of trainees put the handy billy on back to front (or so we thought) so that they were heaving forward instead of aft. It was actually simpler and safer that way, so we changed it round and that's the way we've done it ever since.

'I've never had a bunch of trainees who had a bad voyage. Sure, they might be seasick for three days, but they have a sense of victory once they overcome that. Some mixes of trainees might click together better than others, but that's something that the crew members notice, not the trainees. The young people don't have anything to compare their voyage with; for them it's a unique experience. There might be occasions when the crew begin to think, "This isn't such a hot voyage." It's amazing how just a little more effort at that point can suddenly lift everything and make it work.

'The golden rule is that everybody should go home happy. I think it's up to the crew to set the tone by having a positive attitude right from the word go. It's important to have a big bright smile on arrival day and make everyone feel welcome. I want the trainees to feel comfortable with their environment sooner rather than later. Not *too* comfortable, though. The trick is in thinking up challenges every day which are demanding but achievable. It's a kind of risk management.

'We never risk injury to the trainees or damage to the ships, but we want there to be a sense of risking the achievement or non-achievement of various tasks. It's not a complacent

Master Steve Gamble first sailed on board the **Spirit of Adventure** *as a 15-year-old in 1977.*

sort of happiness we're after; it's the deeper satisfaction that comes from achieving tough goals.

'Young people can cope with adversity remarkably well when they're given a chance. On one recent voyage we had to send a girl off because her father was dying. She was very brave about it and the other trainees were tremendously supportive. Some of them said to me that I must have found it hard breaking the news and, yes, I certainly did. I was touched that they were sensitive to my position as well as the girl's. That group really bonded together and looked after one another. It turned out that there were two other trainees on that voyage who had lost parents.

'There was also a rather timid and quiet 15-year-old aboard, who was one of the young people sponsored by the Forestry Corporation. He came from a troubled family background. There had been no power for two months in the house where he'd been living. He had no warm clothes or sleeping bag or anything like that. The other trainees really took care of him and helped to bring him out of his shell and boost his self-confidence. They elected him as a watch officer for the last day's sailing. There were lots of older trainees who could have done the job more easily, but they recognised this boy would benefit more from being given a position of authority, so they decided to support him instead. I felt really proud of them for that.'

Not many people can match Steve's intimate knowledge of the two *Spirit* ships. He's careful to avoid favouring one vessel over the other. 'I like them both,' he says. 'They're both completely safe and seaworthy and you can have a good time on either of them. From a management point of view, the *Spirit of Adventure* is a bit easier, not just because she's smaller and carries fewer trainees, but because her weight to power ratio enables you to motor out of awkward situations very quickly. On the *Spirit of New Zealand* you need to plan everything carefully in advance. You have to be two or three steps ahead all the time. On the other hand, when she's sailing well, the *New Zealand* really moves. It's easier, I think, for trainees to take over on the *Spirit of Adventure*, but then overcoming difficulties is what the trust's all about.

'One of the things I've discovered from travelling is the standing the trust has among other sail training organisations around the world. We're very highly regarded. This became apparent during the Australian bicentennial, for instance. Some of the crews on

The crew for the Spirit of New Zealand*'s first southern voyage (Picton–Dunedin) in January 1987. From left: Steve Gamble (second mate), Taffy Hayward (engineer), Margaret Pidgeon (first mate), Paul Leppington (master), Chris Gillies (cook), John Burgess and John Duder (watch officers).* (John Duder)

the other ships in the Hobart to Sydney race had been together for months, but Nick Hylton managed to come second on the *Spirit of New Zealand* working with a group of trainees who flew into Hobart the day before the race started. You really need to have your act together to do that. The other crews were amazed.'

Opposite: *The* Spirit of New Zealand *on an early voyage on Waitemata Harbour.*
Overleaf: *The* Spirit of New Zealand.

Chapter Ten:
Sailing into the Future

Well-wishers sometimes ask the trust's chairperson Stephen Fisher if a third ship is likely to be purchased in the near future. They equate success with constant expansion. There are other ways, however, of measuring how well the trust is fulfilling its aims.

'The aim has always been to get as many youngsters as possible out on the water. A two-ship regime seems appropriate to the New Zealand market,' says Fisher. 'A three-ship regime is not only beyond our current capabilities but also beyond the requirements of a country this size. We have no intention to increase the fleet. The main responsibility of the trust is to ensure that the existing opportunities continue to be provided in the future. In other words, it's necessary to maintain two vessels in an economically viable mode of operation and to ensure that when the time comes each of those vessels can be replaced.'

Steel ships don't last forever. Their life expectancy is considerably less than wooden vessels. In April 1993, Curly Hayter, the manager of Vos & Brijs, talked to the Auckland-based magazine *Boating Quarterly* about ship-building methods in the 1970s. He was thinking in particular about the *Spirit of Adventure*. 'These days you can expect a steel ship to last 35 to 40 years,' he said, 'but back in the seventies builders thought the boat would be a write-off after 20 years. Steel boats rust from the inside out, because that's where you get condensation and can't reach it. So it's more important to protect the inside than the outside. In the 1970s that was expensive and it wasn't looked upon as a priority.'

Nowadays the inside of the hull is sandblasted and given a protective coating of zinc and epoxy. When the *Spirit of New Zealand* was built in 1986, using these methods, her life expectancy was estimated at 30 years. Formerly a successful engineering company manager, Bill McCook took over as the trust's operations director (now chief executive) while the *Spirit of New Zealand* was still being commissioned. Like everyone else, he was pleased with progress on the new ship, but he was concerned about the *Spirit of Adventure* and thus he requested an in-depth survey from the Royal New Zealand Naval Dockyard to check the condition of the ship. Was she still an asset to the trust or would she soon prove a liability? How much needed to be spent on her and would it make economic sense to do so?

The rigging was fine, having recently been upgraded as part of ongoing maintenance, and the hull was judged to be in good shape, but some of the engineering and most of the electrics and fittings clearly needed attention. The ship returned to the slipway at Vos & Brijs (now owned by Sanford Ltd) for a major refit. When the builders raised the floor, however, they discovered that the hidden hullplates and the tops of the holding tanks for water, fuel and sewerage were seriously corroded as a result of the less rigorous approach to interior protection in the 1970s.

Over the next four years, the hullplates were gradually replaced and given full protective

Left: *Bill McCook, chief executive of The Spirit of Adventure Trust since 1986.* **Right:**

Engineer Snow Parker in the Spirit of New Zealand's engine room. (Donna MacIntosh)

coating. In 1989 the forward section of the ship was rebuilt to change it from two cabins of, respectively, 9 and 16 hammocks, lying aft of each other, to two equally sized cabins, each containing 13 hammocks, on either side of the ship. The following year, the entire aft section was replaced when holes appeared in the hull during sandblasting.

Needless to say, these alterations and improvements were expensive. More than $1.3 million has been spent on refitting the *Spirit of Adventure* since 1986. The Lottery Grants Board allocated $500,000 in 1989, and the ASB Trusts donated $585,700 towards refurbishment costs in August 1992. Waari Ward-Holmes, the deputy chairman of the ASB Trusts, said at the time that losing the *Spirit of Adventure* would be 'rather like losing part of the adventurous spirit of young New Zealand itself. If the Spirit of Adventure trustees had made the decision to scrap and replace the vessel, I believe the ex-trainees would have been screaming for them to be keelhauled, flogged or whatever they do to recalcitrant sailors these days.'

Today the ship is as near as possible to an 'as new' condition, with the $1.3 million expenditure comparing favourable with the nearly $5 million cost of replacement.

Realistically, however, the trustees know that sooner or later both ships will be beyond refurbishing and newer vessels will need to take their place. The economic life of the *Spirit of Adventure* is now estimated as being approximately a further 15 years and that of the *Spirit of New Zealand* as about 25 years. 'We can't ever become complacent,' says Stephen Fisher. 'We need to set in motion now fund-raising schemes that will guarantee our future. In our twenty-first year, the trust has taken two funding initiatives to see us into the twenty-first century.'

Left: *In 1992 the* Spirit of Adventure *underwent a major refit at the Vos & Brijs shipyard. Among those working on the stripped-down deck are (from left at back): relieving engineer Wyn Ashmore, senior mate Neil Rowarth and permanent engineer Kevin Ralphs; with Voyager Troy Evans and chief executive Bill McCook in the immediate foreground.*

Right: *Longboarding the hull of the* Spirit of Adventure.

One of these is the creation of a new investment fund known as the Spirit of Adventure Foundation. Life members of the foundation, who can be either individuals or corporations, are required to invest $1500 per annum for a period of six years. In return, they each receive Supporters Club membership for six years, a sailing for two aboard one of the vessels, the right to nominate a young person for a leader management six-day programme at a 20 per cent discount, mementoes such as inscribed photographs of the vessels, and an advertising programme whereby the $1500 can be tax-deductible to businesses. The target is to attract at least 640 life members, with the generated income from the professionally managed investments offsetting the annual operating deficit and providing capital reserves for the future.

In 1993 the trust also purchased the forestry rights to a 200-hectare block of radiata pine in the Rotoehu Forest (on the slopes of the hills north of Lake Rotoehu, about 40 kilometres north of Rotorua, not far from the timber port of Tauranga). The Forestry Corporation of New Zealand Ltd has agreed to provide management and other services free of

A line-up along the Spirit of New Zealand's *lower yard: crew member Hamish Wilson (far right) instructs leader manager participants on stowing the square sails.*

cost for the next 15 years. The trust has the option of selling the plantation back to the Forestry Corporation at any stage in the next 28 years at a time that will coincide with the building of a replacement vessel.

'Come year 15, which is when we'll probably want to replace the *Spirit of Adventure*, the forest at today's prices will be worth several million,' says Stephen Fisher. 'If that doesn't cover the replacement costs entirely, it will certainly go a long way towards doing so.'

As one of the trust board's founding members and its chairperson for the last 17 years, Fisher has devoted much of his adult life to devising fund-raising ideas to keep the *Spirits* seaworthy. He stresses, however, that while trustees must use their entrepreneurial skills to the maximum it's important always to remember that the ultimate aim is not to create profits but to offer learning opportunities to young New Zealanders. As part of the joint venture, the Forestry Corporation has agreed to pay the voyage fees for six secondary school students per year from the Bay of Plenty region. This isn't just a symbolic gesture, it's what the *Spirit* programme is all about. The students selected will be youngsters who otherwise could not afford to sail.

The deal with the Forestry Corporation was officially launched on Monday, 28 February 1994 with an afternoon sail around the Port of Tauranga for mayors and school principals from the Bay of Plenty region on board the *Spirit of Adventure*. This wasn't just a symbolic gesture either. It gave local people a chance to inspect one of the ships. Tom Rogers, the general manager of the Forestry Corporation, even emulated trainees by climbing to the top of the foremast. He said afterwards that it reminded him of his youthful days when he scaled pine trees as a forestry worker, but he quipped that this time the trouble was that there were no branches to break his fall. Meanwhile, the trainees who would ordinarily have been on board the *Spirit of Adventure* spent part of the day in Rotorua learning about forest fire-fighting techniques.

To keep the *Spirit* programme afloat, fundraising has to be an unceasing activity. Many of the donations are made quietly, without any media attention. 'We couldn't survive without the steady support of individuals and the business community,' says Bill McCook, the trust chief executive. 'Large companies will often give us special deals when it comes to refitting. Some of the smaller businesses contribute by running accounts for us. It all helps. Every year Stars Marine Ltd donates new outboards for the dinghies. Gifts like that are much appreciated.'

Because of their unique nature, some of the fund-raising initiatives have been widely reported in the national (and, indeed, international) press. On 8 January 1994, for example, the internationally renowned New Zealand soprano Dame Kiri Te Kanawa raised $10,000 for the trust with a twilight concert on the Auckland waterfront. (The sale of limited edition phonecards released to commemorate the concert raised a further $5000.) One of the largest temporary grandstands ever built in New Zealand (eight metres high, with 210 tonnes of scaffolding) was erected on the eastern viaduct basin to accommodate more than 6500 spectators. About 200 others watched from boats, which were assembled in four rows, with the biggest, including the *Spirit of Adventure*, at the back and the smallest in $900 front-row moorings. Dame Kiri's repertoire ranged from arias by Joseph Canteloube and Giacomo Puccini to popular numbers

The Spirit of Adventure Trust has agreed to instruct staff from the Osaka Port Development and Engineering Corporation in its sail training programme. As part of the scheme Satoko Achi, a graduate of Japan's Merchant Marine Academy, served as an officer on board the Spirit of New Zealand *in July 1992. As well as being a first-rate sailor, she is fondly remembered by the* Spirit's *crew and trainees for her good humour and her genius at making paper cranes.* (Norman Smith)

127

like 'Red Sails in the Sunset', George Gershwin's 'Summertime' and the Rod Stewart hit 'Sailing' (which has also been sung by thousands of trainees, over the years, on the decks of the *Spirit* ships).

It was also big news throughout New Zealand in September 1992 when the Osaka Port Development and Engineering Corporation contracted The Spirit of Adventure Trust for a substantial sum to provide a blueprint of the Spirit organisation, including training procedures, ship layouts, instruction manuals, and administration, over a period of three years. Osaka is the third largest city in Japan after Tokyo and Yokohama. Wanting to develop a sail training programme that would encourage young Japanese to work out problems for themselves, the prosperous port company looked around the world for a suitable model and decided that the New Zealand scheme developed by the trust was the best. One of the first Japanese sailors to join a ten-day voyage in New Zealand, Yoshitada Matsubayashi, was quoted in the *New Zealand Herald* as finding the experience 'very enjoyable but hard work'. In August 1993, Pony More, one of the trust's original masters, went to Osaka for three weeks to help prepare the three-masted topsail schooner STS *Akogare* (the name is Japanese for 'yearning for freedom') for her first intake of trainees. Simultaneously acting as sailing adviser, rigging expert and goodwill ambassador, More assisted in sea trials around the islands of southern Japan.

Stephen Fisher is keen to see more exchanges of crew with overseas sail training organisations in the future. He's cautious, however, about accepting the many offers which come to him for the *Spirit of Adventure* or the *Spirit of New Zealand* to take part in tall ship pageants around the world. 'It's a matter of priorities,' he says. 'The needs of our young trainees must come first. Offshore forays are expensive and time-consuming. They're often more limited in the training opportunities they provide than voyages within New Zealand

The trust's 'leader manager' programmes, for young business people aged between 19 and 25, aim to develop basic management and leadership skills by combining the practical experience of sailing the Spirit ships with a series of workshops and simulation exercises.

Above: *Facilitator Bruce Herbert, from the Experiential Training Company, introduces leader manager participants to some fundamental principles in the aft cabin of the Spirit of New Zealand.*

Above: *Sometimes one needs to have faith in others: here a leader manager participant performs the 'trust fall' aboard the Spirit of New Zealand.*

Left: *The relief of having been caught safely is patently obvious!*

Top: *A leader manager participant aloft on* Spirit of New Zealand.

Above: *Cook Hamish Moore, affectionately known as 'Bear', supervises chores in the* Spirit of New Zealand *galley.*

Left: *A leader manager group participates in Relationship Awareness Training (RAT) on deck.*

waters. The pressure of having to arrive at a destination by a particular date might necessitate a lot of motoring, which greatly reduces the number of team-building tasks available to trainees. Overseas voyages can interrupt the ships' ordinary programmes for a long time, thereby disadvantaging the young New Zealanders that the trust exists for. Occasionally exchange students from other countries have been among the trainees.

'The composition of the trust board has changed since my father began in the early seventies with a group of people who were basically his long-time friends. Since then we've broadened the base by bringing to the table new board members with appropriate business, education or maritime skills. It's important, though, not to forget where we came from. We should never lose sight of the fact that for many of the young people who sail on the *Spirit of Adventure* or the *Spirit of New Zealand*, it's a once-in-a-lifetime opportunity. At bottom, what I believe we provide them with, beyond any sailing know-how, is the chance for self-discovery and self-analysis, enabling them to say to themselves, "This is who I am and this is what I want to do." For many of them, the voyages are turning points in their lives.

'The trust's central objective is to guarantee that our youth development programme continues. That means raising sufficient finance to keep both ships in good repair and to replace them when necessary. I would expect any replacement vessel to be a three-masted ship much like the *Spirit of New Zealand*, but that decision is still 15 years away. Keeping fees within affordable reach of young people from a broad social spectrum is another of our primary duties. But above and beyond the monetary considerations there's our commitment to continuing to provide turning points in the lives of New Zealand's citizens of the future.'

Next page: *A rare sight: the* **Spirit of Adventure** *and* **Spirit of New Zealand** *together in the Bay of Islands.* (Nathan Bilow)

131

Appendix One:
Technical Details of STS 'Spirit of Adventure'

Official number: 349074
Port of registry: Auckland
Built: 1973 by Vos & Brijs of Auckland
Gross registered tonnage: 99.64
Net tonnage: 84.63
Displacement: 120
Length overall (including bowsprit): 33.14 m (108 ft 2 in)
Length overall (excluding bowsprit): 27.44 m (90 ft)
Beam: 6.24 m (20 ft 6 in)
Draft: 3.35 m (11 ft)
Sail area: 518.57 m^2 (5,582 ft^2)
Main engine: 6-cyl Cummings Nt 335M turbo-charged
    diesel 175 kW (235 BHP) @ 1800 RPM
Gear box: Twin disc reverse/reduction
Propeller: Fixed 3-blade bronze
Auxiliaries: 2-cyl & 3-cyl Lister diesels each with
    a 16.25 kVA alternator
Maximum speed: 9 knots (power), 11 knots (sail)
Complement (maximum): 9 crew and 26 trainees

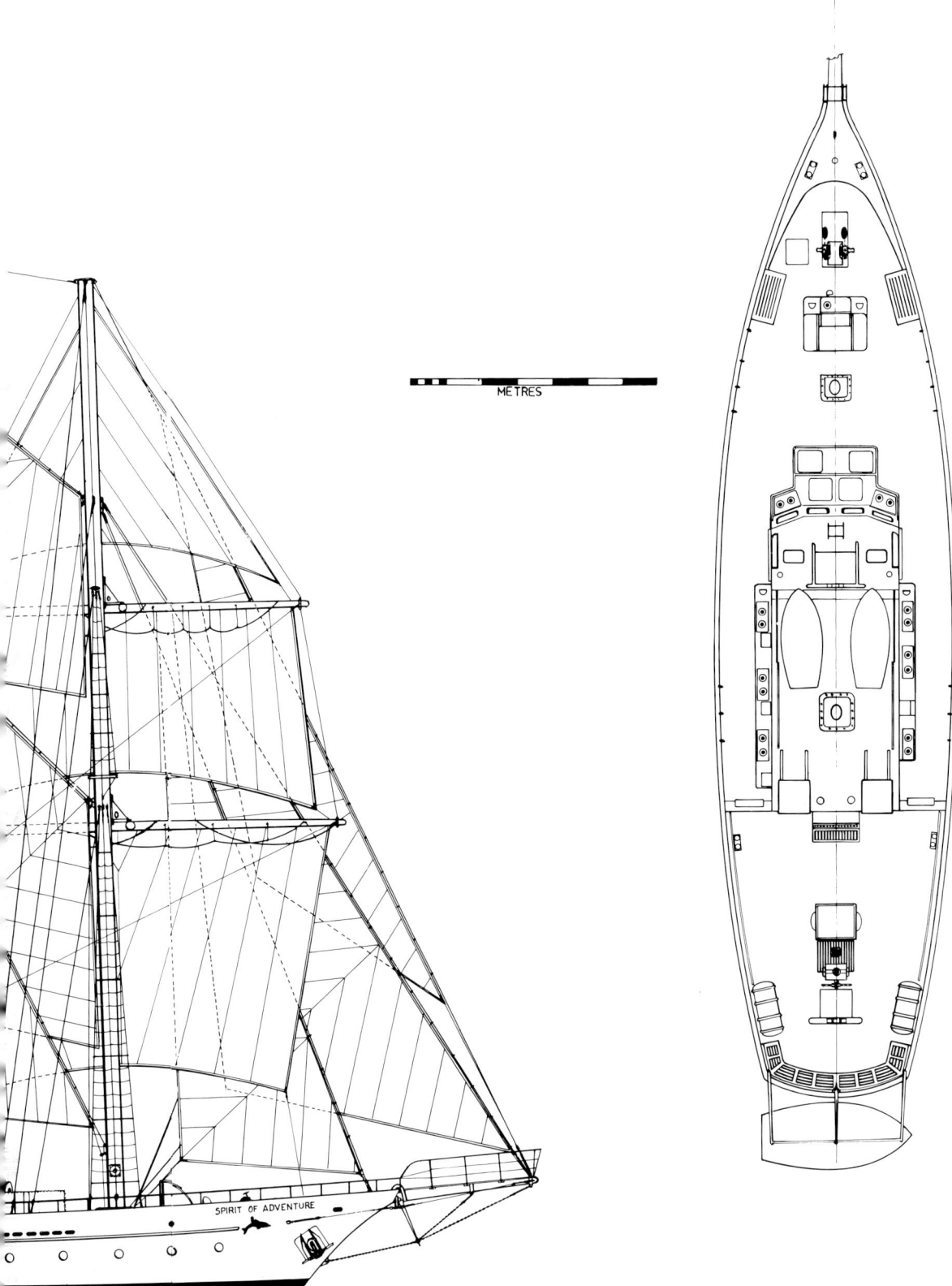

METRES

SPIRIT OF ADVENTURE

Appendix Two:
Technical Details of STS 'Spirit of New Zealand'

Official number: 875169

Port of registry: Auckland

Built: 1986 by Thackwray Yachts Ltd and
The Spirit of Adventure Trust, Auckland

Gross registered tonnage: 184

Net tonnage: 155.32

Displacement: 224

Length overall (including bowsprit): 45.2 m
(148 ft)

Length overall (excluding bowsprit): 33.25 m
(109 ft)

Beam: 9.1 m (29 ft 10 in)

Draft: 3.45 m (13 ft 8 in)

Sail area: 724.3 m^2 (7,965 ft^2)

Main engine: Gardner 8L 3 B
diesel, 250 BHP

Gear box: 828S Tonanko

Propeller: CP14MR three
blade fully feathering

Auxiliaries: Cummins with
40 kVA alternator

Maximum speed: 9 knots
(power), 14 knots (sail)

Complement (maximum):
12 crew and 42 trainees

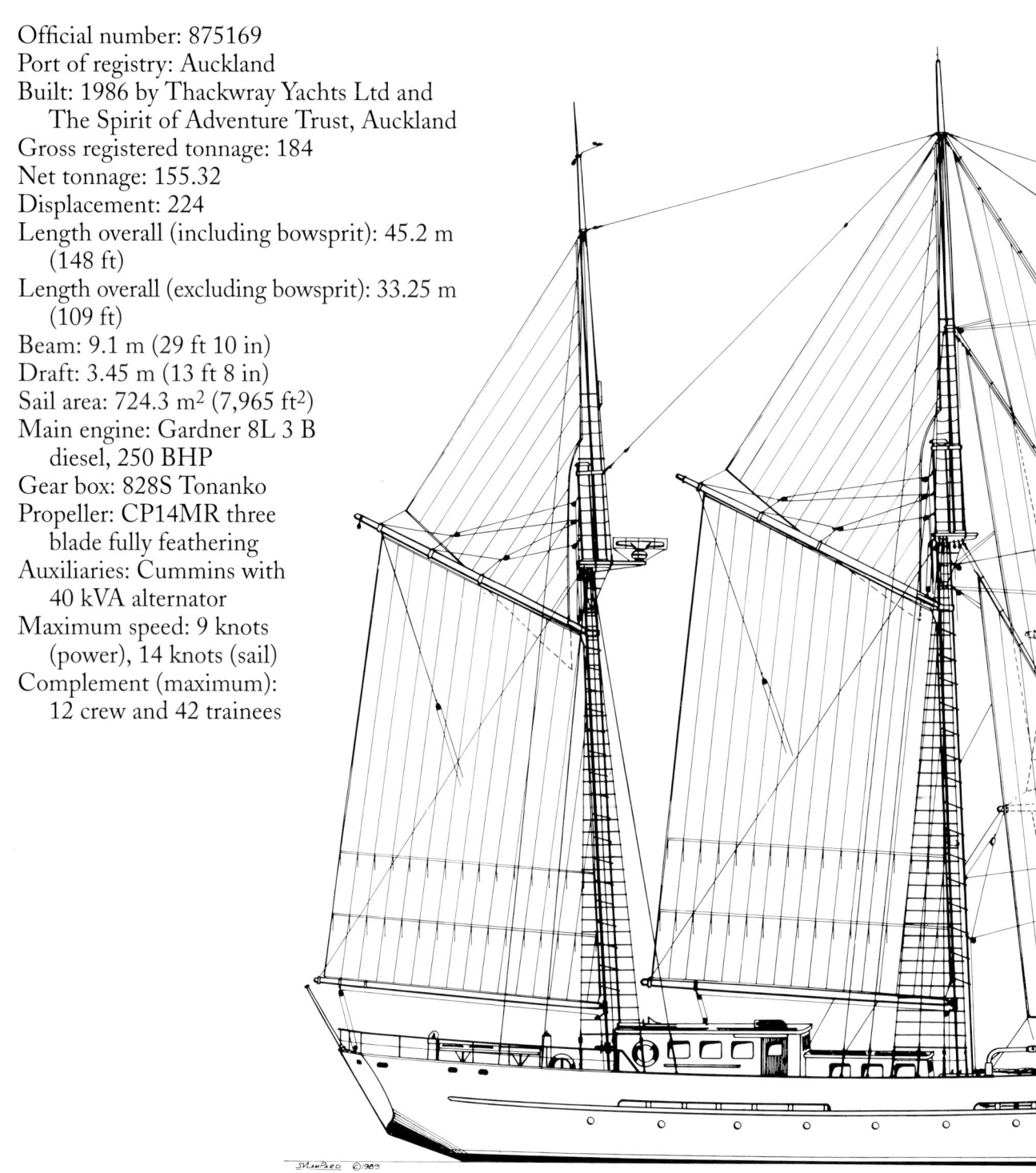

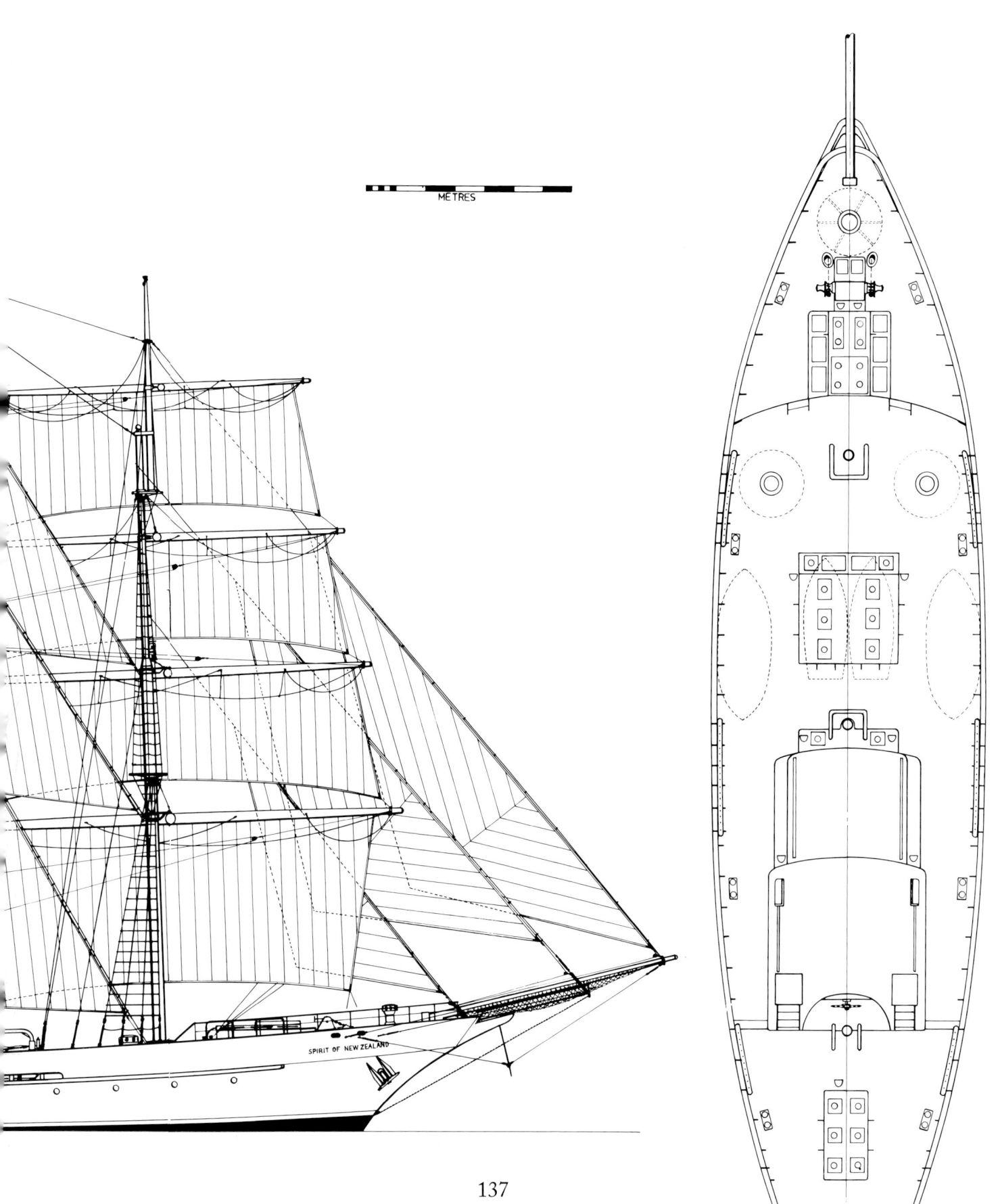

METRES

SPIRIT OF NEW ZEALAND

137

Appendix Three:
The Spirit of Adventure Trust

Patron

Her Excellency Dame Catherine Tizard, GCMG, DBE
Governor General of New Zealand

Vice-Patrons

Hon. Sir David Beattie, GCMG, GVCO, QC
Admiral Sir Gordon Tait, KCB, DSC
Vice Admiral S.F. Teagle

TRUST BOARD

Chairman

Stephen B. Fisher QSO, company director

Deputy Chairman

Captain C. Barry Thompson, RD, marine consultant

Board Members

John N. Duder, civil engineer, company director
Tessa Duder OBE, writer
Fred Huddleston, chartered accountant
John King, lawyer
Noel Robinson, company director
Captain Jim T. Varney, marine consultant
Penny Whiting MBE, sailing school director

Honorary Auditors

Coopers & Lybrand (auditors)

Honorary Solicitors

Russell, McVeagh, McKenzie, Bartleet & Co. (legal)

Honorary Advisors

Dr Dean Campbell (medical)
Kevin O'Sullivan (fire safety)
Brother Pat Lynch (education)
Jarden Morgan Investment Services Ltd (investment)
Curly Hayter (structural engineering)
John Scott (mechanical engineering)
Ogilvy & Mather (advertising and public relations)
Chris Close (computers)
Tom Webster (electrical)

Appendix Four:
Permanent Staff and Crew

Chief executive	Bill McCook
Purser	Patti Rose
Senior master	Paul Leppington
Masters	Bill Curry, Steve Gamble
Cook	Mike Webster
Engineers	Snow Parker, Colin Skudder
National fundraiser	Vaughan Robertson
Administation assistants	Valerie Holmes, Tanya Eyre, Sandra Shaw
Bosun	Bill Morris
Mates	Tim Rynd, Rachel Keown, Alex Date, Deanna Douglas, Vimal Choy
Volunteer co-ordinator	Adrienne Welch
Cadets	Charlotte Orpen, Kent Smith, Catherine Swan, Andy Grocott

The Spirit of Adventure Trust
Operations Office
P.O. Box 2276
Auckland
New Zealand

Appendix Five:
Port Contacts

Whangarei	Peter and Rona McConachy
Tauranga	Bruce Graham
Gisborne	Cynthia Dobson
Napier	Alan Crabbe
New Plymouth	Ray Egarr
Wellington	John Reeve
Picton	David Barnes
Nelson	Warwick Biggs
Lyttelton	Fergus Campbell MBE, RD
Timaru	Court Hobday
Dunedin	Roy Freeland
Bluff	Tom Sawyer

Appendix Six:
Volunteer Crew, 1990–94

Neil Abbott, Keith Adams, Roger Adamson, Robert Alexander, Michael Allen, Garry Allport, Deborah Anderson, Graeme Anderson, Ruth Anderson, Charles Armstrong, Jill Armstrong, Capt. Mike Austin, Lynne Baldwin, Peter Baldwin, Ian Bamford, Capt. Michael Barnett, Dr Graham Barrell, Julie Batchelor, Gary Baxter, John Beavon, Jan Bebbington, Ken Bedford, Dawn Behague, Christopher Behnam, Rowan Bell, Cathy Bendig, Graham Bennett, David Benson-Pope, Richard Berg, Dr Johann Bernhardt, Warwick Biggs, Ron Bird, Bruce Birnie, Stuart Birnie, Sharon Birss, Michael Bishop, Ron Blackman, Antonius Blijlevens, Hazel Blowers, Michael Blowers, Andy Blyth, John Boak, Peter Boniface, Neil Bonner, Margaret Bonnington, Michael Bourke, Glenn Bowden, Dorothy Bowie, Anne Bowmar, David Bradley, Michael Bramley, Mike Breen, Linda Brett, Paul Brimecombe, Barrie Brookes, Standish Brookes, Alan Broomfield, Jean Broomfield, Jack Brunner, Christopher Budgen, John Burgess, Jennifer Burt, Kenneth Burt, Jennifer Butcher, Nancy Caddy, Tracey Calder, Michael Calver, Ewen Cameron, Ian Cameron, Henry Campana, Andrew Campbell, Fergus Campbell, Des Carey, Toni-Maree Carnie, Bruce Carr, John Carruthers, Simon Carryer, Susana Carryer, Paul Carter, Louise Cato, Paul Chaplin, Rebecca Chapman, Martin Cherry, Marion Chisnall, Roger Chisnall, John Church, Jack Churchouse, Judy Clapperton, Leslie Clarke, Simon Cleaver, Valerie Clifford, Christopher Close, Philippa Collins, Alex Conte, Barry Cook, Thomas Cooke, David Cooper, Tony Cooper, Geoffrey Copping, Lewis Cormack, David Cory, Dennis Cottle, Alan Crabbe, Charles Crawford, Grant Crawford, Scott Crawford, Lt. Cdr. Terry Creagh, Tanya Cresswell, Daryl Crocker, Adrienne Crowe, Peter Crowe, Sonia Crowley, Donald Crum, Tony Cummings, Alison Cunningham, Gillian Dacey, Russell Dahlenburg, Norman Dancy, Graeme Darroch, Alan Davenport, Richard Davey, Forrester Davidson, Trevor Davis, Keith Day, Renata Dealy, John Debney, John Dempster, Joan Dickson, William Donaldson, Matthew Dooher, John Downie, Jim Drury, John Duder, Lisa Duder, Tessa Duder, Robert Duffy, Michael Duncan, Darryl Dunford, Darren Dwyer, Janine Dyce, John Dykes, Corrine Eaddy, Alexander Eason, Joanna Eastwood, Alison Edwards, Eric Edwards, Marc Eichblatt, John Elderton, Bryce Ellis, Michael Elwood-Smith, Trevor Erikson, Richard Etheridge, Suzanne Evans, Humphrey Ewens, Trent Fearnley, Lindsay Fenwick, Peter Fisher, Michele Flanagan, Helen Fletcher, Gerald Fogarty, Robert Fogg, Patrick Foot, Mike Foster, Michael Fowler, Peter Fowles, Graham Francis, Ian Francis, Gary Fraser, Jeana Freeman, Robert Freeman, Dr James Frew, Graham Frith, Anna Fulford, David Gall, Brent Gallagher, Thomas Galletly, Nigel Gallienne, Fiona Gannaway, Graham Garden, Chris Garey, Guy Garey, Neil Geerkens, Ian Gilmour, Trish Glasson, Dr Michael Glen, Ian Godkin, Lyn Goldsworthy, Jim Goodsir, Judith Goodsir, John Goodwin, Amanda Gordon, Selina Gordon, Tim Gorter, Debbie Gould, Bruce Graham, Gary Graham, Margaret Graham, Malcolm Grant, Samual Grau, David Griffith-Jones, Valerie Griffith-Jones, Robin Grigg, William Grindlay, Joseph Grundy, Fiona Gunn, George Gunn, Thomas Guthknecht, Desmond Gyde, David Hagen, Reginald Hall, Toni Halliday, Aaron Halstead, Donald Hamer, Frances Hammond, Keith Hammond, Donald Handley, Rex Hannam, Wolfgang Harder, John Hardwick, Andrew Harris, Susan Harrison, Melissa Haskell, Jean Hatch, Robert Hawkins, Trevor Hawkins,

Geoffrey Hebditch, Christine Heffer, Francis Helps, Lewis Henderson, Kris Henley, Kristian Henley, Bryan Hensley, Robert Henwood, Barrie Herlihy, David Herrington, Robyn Hetherington, John Hillery, Kathleen Hoare, Court Hobday, Katharine Holdsworth, Darren Holland, Martin Holland-Kearins, Alfred Holst, Brian Horrocks, Donald Hounsell, Ian Howden, Thomas Hoy, Norma Hudson, Robert Hudson, Geoff Hughes, James Hughes, David Humpherson, Capt. Rick Hunter, David Hutcheson, Capt. Nick Hylton, Capt. Gib Inkster, Alexander Innes, Justine Irwin, Dennis Jackson, Helen Janzen, James Jeffery, Adrienne Jensen, Bruce Johns, Edward Johnson, Catherine Johnstone, Suzanne Jolly, Bruce Jones, Paul Jukes, David Jury, John Kearns, Damien Kelly, James Kelly, Trevor Kenworthy, Annette Keogh, Rachel Keown, Dennis Kestila, Dorothy Kestila, Owen Key, Won-Lee Kiew, Graham King, Sandra King, James Kinghorn, Stanley Kirkpatrick, Janette Kirkup, Barbara Kissock, John Klingenberg, Peter Knaapen, Allan Kneale, Tony Kortens, Slawomir Kunz, Christopher Laird, Ross Lamb, Tania Lamberton, Robyn Lamont, Michael Lampard, Brien Lampen-Smith, Jim Lane, Jill Larsen, Poul Lauritzen, Andrew Lawrence, Fiona Laws, Martin Layzell, Brigitte Lecren, Robert Lee, Michael Leeves, Marshall Lefferts, Lynne Lever, Georgina Lewis, Dr Philippa Leys, Capt. Andrew Lidgard, John Liell, Garry Linkhorn, Capt. Murray Lister, John Lock, Donald Lockie, Gary Lokum, Thomas Look, Christopher Lordan, James Lott, Karin Lott, David Lourie, Robert Lourie, Julie Lovelock, Richard Lovering, David Lowe, Christopher Lowman, Craig Lucena, Jody Lusk, Shane Luzak, Graeme Lyons, Alister MacAlister, Terry Macartney, Sarah MacKenzie, Wayne MacKenzie, Alistair MacLean, Donald MacLean, Dr Frank MacNamara, Martin Mallow, John Marer, Kenneth Marshall, Richard Marshall, Doris Martin, Claire Martinez, Helen Martinez, Peter Mason, Paul Matthews, Robin Maunsell, Geoffrey Maurice, Keith Maydon, Alan Mayne, Gillian Mayo, Helen McArthur, Rosemary McAuley, John McCaffery, Christopher McCallum, Hugh McCarroll, Peter McConachy, Rona McConachy, James McConchie, Yvonne McCrystal, Murray McGregor, Jane McIlroy, Russell McIntosh, Dawn McIntyre, Robert McIntyre, Elle McKay, Donald McKelvey, Paul McLaren, Sue McNatty, David McNickle, David McPherson, Denis McQueen, Catherine Mead, Sonya Meek, Prue Meister, Alfred Memelink, Selina Merrick, Sterling Meyer, Bill Millen, Anne Miller, Tony Miller, Anthony (Jim) Mills, Heather Mills, Quentin Mitchell, Tracey Mitchell, Gael Mockford, Max Moffatt, Alan Molloy, Andrew Moore, John Moore, Kerry Moore, Roderick Moore, Lennox Mounsey, Charles Mountfort, Hamish Muir, Beverely Munro, Capt. Hugh Munro, Kelvin Munro, Graham Murray, Rosemary Musters, Murray Nattrass, Stephen Neale, David Neil, Richard Neutze, Warren Neville, Alison Newbald, Geordie Nicholson, James Nimmo, David Noon, Christopher Nordstrom, John Norman, Christopher Northmore, Kevin O'sullivan, Russell Oliver, Christopher Ollivier, Jennie Ormsby, Di Osborne, Derek Oud, C Overy, Kay Paget, Kym Park, Trevor Payton, Melvyn Pearson, Mike Pearson, Brian Peek, Kim Penny, Jane Penton, Claire Pepper, Cdr. Norman Perrett RN (Retd), Capt. Peter Petherbridge, Zena Petherbridge, Tina Pick, Margaret Pidgeon, Bruce Pigou, Karen Pinkney, Peter Plaistowe, Heather Pohl, Peter Pole, Denis Port, Leslie Porter, Colin Potter, Pierce Prendergast, Nigel Prior, Stephen Punter, John Quaife, Barry Rance, Clare Rance, Helen Rance, Capt. Ian Rankin, Ian Rankin, Richard Raudon, Andrea Raves, Kevin Redden, Roger Redmond, Nicola Rees, John Reeve, Michael Renshaw, Tony Revel, Joanne Richards, Josephine Richards, Victor Richards, Peter Ridge, Capt. Tim Ridge, Brett Riley, Julie Riley, Lewis Rivers, Anthony Roberton, Grant Roberts, Capt. Jennifer Roberts, Maurice Robertson, Trevor Robertson, Rowena

Robinson, Anthony Rodgers, Colin Rodgers, Newell Rogers, Patrick Rogers, Heath Ronald, Michael Rossouw, Capt. Geoffrey Rowarth, Dr Jacqueline Rowarth, Capt. Neil Rowarth, Arthur Rowlands, Mary Rowlands, Georgina Ruffell, Loretta Ruissen, Paul Rusden, Kim Rutter, Tim Rynd, Beth Rypstat, Francis Sail, Paul Salter, Ivor Sanders, Terry Sanders, Eric Sands, Rachel Sanson, Charles Satterthwaite, David Saunders, Tom Sawyer, Patrick Scelly, Murray Scott, Peter Scott, Lynne Scrymgeour, Avrael Semple, Christine Shardlow, Mary Sharp, David Shearman, Dawn Short, Katherine Short, Duane Shute, Stephen Signal, Alasdair Sime, Deborah Simmiss, Peter Sinclair, Geoff Sivess, Ian Skene, Alison Skinner, Stuart Slack, Jaap Slagter, Barbara Smith, Brian Smith, Kent Smith, Murray Smith, Nevada Smith, Rex Smith, Ross Smith, Roy Smith, Susan Soltysik, Gaynor Spiers, Ricky Spiers, Stanley Spiers, Rhyl Stafford, John Stent, Guy Stephens, Hugh Stevens, Stella Still, Hans-Dieter Stoltenberg, Heather Stone, Margareth Stumpel, Stuart Sturge, Kevin Such, Amanda Swan, Glenys Swan, Capt. Roy Swan, Dr Michael Tarttelin, Andrew Taylor, Bridgit Taylor, Ivan Taylor, John Taylor, Peter Taylor, Sheena Taylor, Andrea Thode, Capt. Con Thode, Aneurin Thomas, Celia Thomas, Donald Thomas, Kerry Thomas, Leonard Thompson, Jay Thompson-Milne, Judith Tizzard, Graham Toomer, Judy Trafford, Blair Trask, Adrian Turner, John Turnwald, John Turpin, Warren Tyer, Brendon Vallings, Tom Van Aalst, Erwin Van Asbeck, Mark Van Dam, Peter Van Der Beek, Capt. Jim Varney, Deidre Vellenoweth, Michael Vining, Annabel Vining-Pretty, John Vrolyk, Felicity Walbran, Gregory Walker, Capt. Alan Wallis, Sally Wallis, Chris Walsh, David Ward, Mary Warr, Sarah Watchman, Douglas Watkins, Janet Watkins, Peter Watkins, Anthony Watson, David Watt, William Watt, Janet Wattam, Graham Weakley, Edward Wealleans, Capt. Ian Webb, Jillian Webster, Capt. Richard Webster, Adrienne Welch, Bruce Wenzlick, Valentine Were, Frances Wharry, Todd Wheeler, Mark Whelan, Barbara White, Grant White, Robyn White, William White, Paul Whitehouse, Capt. Brian Whiteman, Jack Whitworth, Chrissy Wickes, Alan Wighton, Co Wijchers, Brian Williams, Eric Williams, Maree Williams, Mary Williams, Mathew Williams, John Wills, Linda Wills, Robert Willyams, Hamish Wilson, Ian Wilson, John Wilson, David Withers, Pearl Wojak, Christopher Wood, Elena Wright, Kristeen Yelavich, Stuart Young, Robyn Zink.

143